DREAMING BIG IN CHINA

By Lu Yang

新世界出版社
NEW WORLD PRESS

First Edition 2009

By Lu Yang Et al.
Translated by Yang Yaohua Et al.
Edited by Li Shujuan
Cover Design by Wang Tianyi

ISBN 978-7-80228-841-6

Published by
NEW WORLD PRESS
24 Baiwanzhuang Street, Beijing 100037, China

Distributed by
NEW WORLD PRESS
24 Baiwanzhuang Street, Beijing 100037, China
Tel: 86-10-68995968
Fax: 86-10-68998705
Website: www.newworld-press.com
E-mail: frank@nwp.com.cn

Printed in the People's Republic of China

Preface

Chinese or foreigner, each one has a dream which he or she strives to realize.

On August 8, 2008, when the Olympic torch was lit in the Bird's Nest (the National Stadium), China's long-cherished Olympic dream finally came true. The Olympic slogan "One World, One dream" had already become familiar in the streets of Beijing, and "Welcome to Beijing" became the most frequently used catch phrase of the city in 2008.

This year, 2008, was also a year for foreigners to build, seek and realize their dreams, and Beijing was the place where their dreams came true, which could be seen from the many world and Olympic records that were broken.

The world will never forget the scene at the Olympic opening ceremony, when 3,000 young Chinese men appeared dressed as Confucius's 3,000 disciples and reading the sage's *Analects*. One of the famous sayings from the *Analects*, "Far and near, we are one family," resounded over the Bird's Nest, showing Chinese hospitality to friends from afar. At the Olympic Games people found that China was an ideal place to realize their dreams.

Hospitality has been a Chinese tradition for thousands of years. The Olympic athletes and tourists in China all felt the sincerity of their hosts. Many athletes held banners reading, "Thank you, China," and many tourists used different ways to express their thanks and favorable impressions to the Chinese people. Despite the disastrous snowstorm and distressing earthquake in China earlier in the year, and the inhospitality shown during the torch relay outside the Chinese mainland, the Chinese people still welcomed and received friends from all around the world with sincerity. "The world used to wait for China to integrate, but today China is patiently waiting for the world to get to know her," said Fu Ying, Chinese ambassador to Britain.

Every person who has visited China, either for a quick tour or a long stay, can sense China's dramatic changes, which have taken place in the past 30 years of reform and opening-up, as long as an objective view is taken. The biggest developing nation in the world, in spite of certain problems and imperfections, is young, vigorous and hopeful. This vast land of 9.60 million square kilometers may be not rich enough, but it is a place suitable for planting dreams. And quite a few wise people have already harvested fruits which have by no means a lower value than Olympic medals.

In the initial stage of the reform and opening-up, the "American dream" and "Japanese dream" tempted many Chinese to go overseas. But now some of them have come back. Many foreigners have also found that in China they could also design their life and realize their dreams. "Chinese dream" is not listed in everyday vocabulary yet, but whether it will become a frequently used word is a matter for conjecture. Many Chinese went abroad, learned advanced technology and ideas there, and returned to build careers in China. These people have formed a distinct social group—the overseas-educated. Likewise, many foreigners have come to China with their dreams and love for Chinese culture. Indeed, some have taken China as their homeland. Isn't this the charm of the "Chinese dream"?

Western countries are too developed to have enough opportunities for improvement. Compared to them, developing countries offer more opportunities and challenges. Take China, for example. Her unprecedented changes over the last 30 years have brought to both the nation and individuals a host of possibilities for development. The overseas-educated, foreigners and native Chinese are all citizens of the global village, and are facing unprecedented chances. We hope that all the people tilling this land will reap a good harvest.

This book continues the genre of *Living in China*. The authors interviewed 19 foreign friends who study or work in China, and was touched and edified by their stories about their different Chinese dreams, big and small. Some of those dreams have been realized, while others are still in progress. Their stories show different experiences and life values, and reflect some of the realities of today's China. In fact, people who have lived in China for a while are more authoritative about what kind of a country China is and what kind of a nation the Chinese people are. We, as well as the foreign friends interviewed, cherish the common with that their stories may help friends from all around the world have a better understanding of new China, fill the gaps in the global village and melt the ice between different peoples.

In 2008 the Chinese people came to realize that there was a disturbingly thick wall between China and the rest of the world. However, when they saw the astronauts of the Shenzhou VII spacecraft walking in outer space they were convinced that any barrier could be overcome. Why not go and ask those foreigners living and working in China? They may give you the correct answer, because in China they can feel that a new sun rises every day, and dreams are being realized every day.

Lu Yang
October 5, 2008

Contents

Personal File

Name: Johan Björkstén

Chinese Name: Dalong (Big Dragon)

Nationality: Swedish

Occupation: TV Host, entrepreneur

Time in China: 17 years

Big Dragon's Sky

Dalong likes a hectic life. The young Swede first came to China because he was fascinated by the country's fabulous dynamism. He was interested in China's language and culture, but mainly wanted to start his own business in an exciting new market. At the time, he probably never imagined that his outgoing, humorous personality would end up making him a local TV and showbiz celebrity. Today, he is famous even in PR business circles for his ability to bring fun and cheerfulness to work. People tend to enjoy themselves when Dalong is around. I personally suspect that he left Sweden because his own country was simply not exciting enough for him. He came to China just to "join the fun".

*H*e speaks such excellent Chinese that he can quote classical citations and poetry by heart, and he easily holds his own even in fierce debates with the most glib professional Chinese TV anchors. He has written several textbooks on the language. But his accomplishments in the business field are even more extraordinary: Dalong has founded three companies, was a co-founder of the Swedish Chamber of Commerce in China and has managed to find time to write books on management and communications, in addition to managing his own businesses. He has a dream: "I cannot become Chinese, but I hope one day to be an honorary Beijing citizen."

Grass doesn't grow on a well-traveled road

Many music lovers still remember Dalong's radio shows featuring Scandinavian music. At a time when China was just opening up to foreign music and culture, listeners broadened their visions to an unfamiliar realm of music. Later, he hosted his own music show on Beijing TV, and taught cooking on the popular program "I Love Western Food." CCTV and many provincial TV stations have invited him to host their programs.

I saw Dalong for the first time on a TV sports program, acting as interpreter for Jan-Ove Waldner, the leading Swedish table tennis player and a local megastar. China is "the Kingdom of Table Tennis", and Waldner was here to meet local fans. For almost two decades he had played against seven generations of top Chinese players. He won gold medals in the men's singles events in all major events, including the Olympics. He was the first "grand slam" winner in the world. No other non-Chinese player has reached the same level, and in China only Liu Guoliang and Kong Linghui have won as many medals as Waldner. His strong spirit, never admitting defeat, together with unexpected tactics and unique skills, earned him a reputation for being a "guerrilla leader". Later, when he continued to outperform generation after generation of Chinese opponents, he became known by the respectful nicknames of Lao Wa: *Old Waldner and The Evergreen.*

Waldner always creates a great sensation wherever he goes in China. But on the TV show, my attention was captured by his young and lively interpreter. With his accurate and vivid translation, plus an ad-lib remark now and then, Dalong raised the level of the show from a regular sports interview to a lively and cheerful meeting with a beloved sports icon. I especially noticed Dalong's Chinese idiomatic vocabulary and flawless pronunciation; if you closed your eyes, you would never have been able to tell that this was a fair-haired, blued-eyed foreigner speaking.

Actually, I also noticed that his "golden hair" was not that thick any more, as he was getting a bit bald on top. This was a bit out of keeping with his sunny, young face, and reminded me of an oft-quoted remark by Ge You, the bald Chinese movie star: "Grass doesn't grow on a well-traveled road."

Chinese people like smart guys. That may be one explanation why

Dalong is so popular in China. Da Shan, a well-known comedian from Canada, is usually quoted as the model of foreign students learning Chinese; "Your Chinese is as good as Da Shan's" is the highest complement on fluency in the language. So I was very surprised when I first heard Dalong on television. My first thought was that "here is a guy who speaks even better than Dashan." But Dalong's faultless Mandarin is just one facet of his linguistic talents: In addition to his native Swedish, he is also fluent in English, French, German and Russian. And there is more to his smarts than language: he has a Master of Science in Molecular Dynamics, has dabbled in opera, was the vocalist of his own rock band and has even managed to attain a modest proficiency in Chinese calligraphy. In addition, he has been a successful radio DJ with his own weekly music show, and a skilled amateur chef, having produced and hosted of weekly cooking classes on TV for more than four years, in addition to hosting his own music video and home furnishing shows. Local producers often invite him to host other local programs, as he is known for contributing to high ratings. He has penned well-received books on how to learn and write Chinese, and even written a book, in Chinese, on public relations in China. As the founder and chairman of his latest

Balding Johan looks cool.

venture, Eastwei Relations, a PR consultancy, he is concurrently the vice-chairman of the Swedish Chamber of Commerce in China.

How does he do it, one wonders? "I always try to find gaps and opportunities, whether doing business, writing books or producing TV shows," Dalong says. He is also fiercely competitive, and does his best to be at the top of everything he does.

So is he the most famous Swede in China? Probably, but after Waldner of course. After that TV show I started to pay attention to Dalong, and found that he was a frequent guest on TV shows all over the country. Swedish soccer players Mellberg and Ljungberg are well known among local soccer lovers, but it is hard to judge their popularity outside football circles. Most people in China have little idea of who Carl XVI Gustaf, the King of Sweden, is. But the number of Chinese who know Dalong is probably many times the total population of Sweden.

Behind the celebrity surface is a successful business story. Dalong's entrepreneurial career in China has been mostly smooth, particularly since his Eastwei company was set up. This company is now seen as something of a benchmark for the local PR industry. His book, *PR, Chinese Style*, written in Chinese for local PR practitioners, is seen as the standard textbook by Chinese colleagues, and as a guide to the Chinese market by foreign colleagues. It has been reprinted time and again. Some media reports even claim that Dalong has "reinvented China's PR industry", though he himself has repeatedly stated that there was no "reinvention" to speak of and that he just wanted to put forth some ideas "for people to think about". He is highly regarded for his accomplishments and for his generosity in sharing his experience with others.

Autographing his new book *PR, Chinese Style.*

Not long ago, I met Dalong in his Eastwei office. He hadn't changed much since I first saw him on TV, still wearing the same kind of friendly smile. But I did notice that there had been a tendency for the bald spot to expand. His close-cropped hair added an element of coolness to his scholarly demeanor. The shining forehead seemed more eye-catching than on TV, but he didn't seem self-conscious about this. Asked if early baldness had something to do with family genes, he said it was not related to heredity. "My grandfather was thick-haired and my father's hair is pretty bushy," he said. "My baldness started when I was only a teenager. Grandpa was more than six feet two, and father is a little bit shorter than grandpa but still taller than I. The height and hair thickness of our three generations tend to decrease. "'Stature gets smaller. Hair gets thinner,' Dad used to sigh when I was in my twenties. 'But head gets smarter,' I retorted. 'Not necessarily', Dad shot back."

The smart guy has great originality

In fact, Dalong's father never made light of his son's intelligence. But he may not have foreseen his son's colorful experience which would lead to such a great reputation in China.

Dalong was born in Lund, a university city in Sweden, in 1964, a Year of the Dragon, according to the Chinese calendar. Father, of Finnish origin, and mother, a Swede, are both graduates of the city's university. Dalong has two younger sisters and an adopted younger brother from Korea. A couple of years ago, his recently retired father was working in Estonia. As a well-known professor of pediatrics, his father also travels widely around the world giving lectures. The family hobby of traveling around the world "internationalized" him, Dalong said.

Perhaps his future fame TV host and Radio DJ could also have been foretold from an early age. He manifested this potential even when he was in elementary school. The first graders organized an auction of coffee, bread and biscuits to earn pocket money for extracurricular activities. Little Johan acted as an earnest auctioneer. Gavel in hand, possibly the youngest auctioneer in history, he displayed his ability to take charge of future gatherings and created a long-lasting, untiring conversation topic for his grandmother, which she would recall again and again over the coming years.

Sweden is a beautiful country. As a kid, Dalong would go biking with his father to explore the deep, dense forests. He would also often watch ice hockey, his little hand in Dad's, heartily cheering for his local team while enjoying a hot dog. All these are wonderful childhood memories. But it was also Dad who gave him his first contact with Chinese culture by taking him to a Chinese restaurant at age seven. "As soon as I stepped inside, I was instantly immersed in a rich foreign culture—beautiful calligraphy and paintings, and splendid carved roof beams," he said. "It was so different, so exciting. From that first moment I was immediately interested in the 5,000-year-old culture of this great country." The delicious Chinese food was probably the strongest temptation. After a bit of fiddling around, and some help from the service staff, young Johan learned to wield chopsticks, a skill he later liked to show off to his schoolmates and friends.

But Johan also had early cultural interests. Although his passion for Chinese cuisine has remained to this day, he would also go to museums to see Chinese cultural relics, learning to appreciate Chinese calligraphy and painting. Although he didn't have the chance to study Chinese culture systematically, these early activities laid the preliminary foundation for him to be a future China expert.

Chinese usually call boys of about 14 years old "cubs", conveying a mixed feeling of love and annoyance. We say teenagers can "make devils cry". There are some well-behaved kids, but they are few and far between. I believe teenagers from other countries are probably no better behaved than Chinese kids. In his famous opera "Le Nozze di Figaro", Pierre-Augustin Caron de Beaumarchais describes a young Cherubino as "a kid whom all mothers under heaven would dream of and all mothers under heaven would have a headache with." It shows that "bad people are bad all over the world" and all imps are "mischievous" everywhere.

But at 14, Johan was instead busy setting up his first organization. At

this time he was intensely interested in collecting beer cans. When he had already amassed a sizable collection of different beer brands, he conceived an idea: to form a country-wide association of beer-can collectors to exchange their collectibles and related information. He put an ad in the national newspaper that read "Beer-can collectors! We are forming a beer-can collectors' society. Join now! The first caller to sign up will get three American cans for free…."

Dalong is still unable to conceal his pride when mentioning this event. "I ended up getting 70 calls. I didn't have enough free cans for them, and had to say, 'Sorry, you are too late and all the cans are already gone.' The association did come into being, with 30 members or so. Each member put down 50 Swedish *crowns* (roughly equivalent to 50 Chinese yuan) as the annual membership fee. As the founder, I became Member No. 1 and chairman of the association. Member No. 2 was a man in his fifties, who became treasurer. After a few years, I became occupied with other business, so I left at 20, but the association has been active ever since. I even received a letter in 2003 asking me for a short article to commemorate the 25th Anniversary of The Swedish Beer Can Collectors Society. I was told that membership had expanded to more than 600 people. I guess it may be even larger now."

The establishment of the association was good news to brewers. So before long an association of brewers came over for a get-together. They also had a news reporter on the spot to interview the young chairman. Johan exhibited the quality and ability of a leader while other youngsters of the same age were probably mainly busy making trouble.

But the chairmanship of this society was not the only early sign of the entrepreneurial spirit that would lead to his future business success in China.

Just as in China, compulsory education in Sweden requires nine-year schooling for all children aged seven to 15. Of these children, almost all attend high school. But in the final years of high school, Dalong found a way to beat the system. A Swedish educational law at the time stipulated that if a student found his teacher biased against him, he could sign up for examinations at another school and the grade would still count towards graduation. Having lived for a year in the US, Dalong was confident that he would surely receive an excellent grade in English even if he didn't go to English classes. So he did his exam, received his credits, and was exempted from the English curriculum. While other students were working hard on English, he quietly used this time to similarly finish his German credits and was again exempted from classes. The more he studied, the fewer classes he had to attend, and the more credits he could gain in a leisurely and unhurried way. One after another, Dalong finished his courses in chemistry, biology, social science, philosophy, religious studies, and so on.

I am not sure a teacher would really be "biased" towards such a student, but according to the law, they could have done nothing even if that were the case. Even today, Dalong still clearly remembers his final year high school schedule: no classes Monday; classes from 2 to 5 p.m. Tuesday; classes for the whole day Wednesday; classes from 9 to 12 a.m. Thursday; and absent from class Friday.

This schedule gave him enough time to work on his first entrepreneurial venture. When he was 16, Johan saw a business opportunity in the hand-drawn graphs and charts his father used in scientific publications. So he registered a scientific drawing company, and soon had a pretty solid business going. "At that time personal computers were not widely available. My

company met customer needs for fast and accurate drawing, and we received many orders. I was so busy that I had to hire a helper. My monthly income was larger than that of many adults. As a high school student I could make my own money and that gave me a sense of achievement."

Viking kid braves a new life in Beijing

Johan finished his education at Uppsala University, one of the oldest institutions of higher learning in Europe, having been founded in 1477. There, Johan continued to show his intelligence and wisdom, his linguistic talents in particular.

With a good grounding in English, plus one year's education in an American school, Johan's English is as good as his mother tongue in terms of listening comprehension, speaking, reading and writing. Besides English, he can read French and German with ease. He picked up Russian when he was in a military school for training before attending university. Johan took pleasure in learning Russian, though the trainees were forced to do so. "We had to learn and remember three hundred or four hundred new vocabulary items from a 40-page booklet a week. Every Friday we would take a test translating 80 sentences of Swedish into Russian. You were allowed 15 mistakes on each test. If you failed for three weeks in succession, you would be dismissed from the military academy. When you were dismissed, you would be assigned to the most boring jobs, such as cleaning toilets. You learn fast when you are under such pressure. I managed not to be dismissed, though I was always among the below-average students." It is relatively easy for Western Europeans to learn English, French and German, since many of their words are similar. That's why it is not uncommon for Western Europeans to speak several languages. But as a Slavonic language, Russian is quite different from other European languages in pronunciation and writing, particularly in its complex grammar. But at the military school, Johan and his fellow students were required to become fluent in just one year's time. This military training taught Johan the discipline that would one day make him one of most accomplished foreign speakers and writers of Chinese ever. "Many people say I have a 'talent for languages'," he says, "but learning a language is about many things: pronunciation or musical skills; memory; and analytical or grammar skills, for example. Few people have all of these skills. But the single most important thing is dedication and discipline. Military school taught me that it is actually possible to master a new language in a single year if you are prepared to devote enough effort to it."

He spent two semesters on Chinese in Stockholm. "To be honest, I was a little bit afraid at first," he admitted. "In Western countries, people regard learning Chinese as one of the most difficult things you can do. When people want to describe something really difficult, they will say it is 'harder than learning Chinese'." But the experience gained at the military school helped him a lot: "The first week, we received an 80-page grammar and were told the first examination would be two weeks later. From the army, I was used to having to master the material in time for the exam, so I crammed intensively, only to discover that the exam only covered the first couple of pages. I had learned the entire first semester's grammar by heart."

Clearly, enthusiasm also has something to do with it, and there is no doubting Dalong's enthusiasm for the Chinese language. As he enjoyed his first meals in Chinese restaurant together with his father, he was already fostering an intense interest in this oriental, ancient and mysterious country.

When he grew up, Johan wanted to learn a quite different and unique foreign language from any of the European tongues. His uncle, whom he has always admired, gave him some decisive advice: "You should learn Chinese. Although China is still a developing and backward country, it has great potential. And it is an ancient country with a fascinating history and several thousand years of civilization."

Learning Chinese calligraphy. The first step: tracing in black ink over characters printed in red.

Another important experience in learning Chinese is, according to Johan, to pay attention to pronunciation. "With good pronunciation, it becomes easier to memorize words and sentences, and you will get a lot of positive feedback when you talk to people. This is particularly important in learning a language that is very different from your own," he says. He would rather turn to a tape recording if the teacher's pronunciation is inaccurate. He used to have a Chinese teacher with a heavy Sichuan accent. With that kind of accent, the teacher couldn't make a distinction between "z" and "zh", "c" and "ch" or "s" and "sh". So Johan again left the classroom to study on his own, listening to recorded teaching materials. Even when he first came to China, his oral Chinese was really pleasant to the ear of Chinese people. They were amazed to learn that he had studied Chinese for only one year—and abroad, in Stockholm.

In 1986, he finally had the chance to realize the long-cherished dream of going to China. He found a job as a tour guide, accompanying a group of Swedish tourists to Beijing. But he experienced a mild shock as soon as he got out of Beijing airport. "I arrived for my first visit to Beijing on a particularly torrid summer day. The cab driver asked 50 US dollars for driving me to downtown Beijing—a fortune for a poor student like myself. My experience from other countries told me to haggle with him on the price, though I really didn't know how much I should be paying. I made a deal with him at 15 US dollars. I learned later that I had still been fleeced."

The rest of the visit outweighed the initial loss. The first experience of the scorching Beijing summer was unforgettable. "I stayed in a cheap hostel, charging eight yuan per person for a night in an eight-person dormitory room. The other guests were mainly truckers delivering goods to the capital. Staying in a hostel room with seven Chinese people allowed me to practice the same basic sentences over and over again. With the truckers coming and going, I always had a fresh supply of Chinese teachers—free of charge." In this way, Johan could connect with ordinary Chinese people at a time when China was not yet as open as it is today, while at the same time efficiently improving his oral Chinese.

Johan Björkstén's "official" Chinese name is Bai Shihua—literally "White Stonebirch", a direct translation from the Swedish. But today, almost all Chinese know him by his nickname "Dalong" which is also the artistic name he used on television. This nickname was another important outcome of his first visit. The Chinese tourist guide he worked with gave him the name

"Dalong", which means "Big Dragon", upon learning that Johan was born in 1964, a Year of the Dragon according to the traditional Chinese calendar. But the guide probably didn't expected that this name would have such wide echoes in China later on.

In 1988, Dalong registered as a full-time student at the Department of Chemistry at Peking University, the "Harvard of China". At first, I found it a bit curious why he didn't study at the Department of Chinese. But studying his chosen field of natural science in a Chinese language environment was a way of "killing two birds with one stone" while making friends with Chinese fellow-students.

After finishing his studies at Peking University in 1990, he returned to his alma mater to study mathematics, and in 1992 enrolled as a postgraduate student in the young field of molecular dynamics. He got his Master's degree in 1994, and decided to come back to China instead of pursuing a PhD. He was determined to lead a different life in a very different country, and carve out a new career in Beijing, a city he saw as being full of opportunities. "I always tell young people to live for some time in countries that have different cultures. Even if you are making a living as a dishwasher, that experience will enrich your life and teach you a new way of thinking. I feel as if I have three pairs of intellectual 'eye glasses'—the different perspectives of Sweden, America and China, the countries where I have lived. Through these lenses, I can observe the world from different angles. That makes it possible to enlarge our horizons and understand how other people think, doesn't it?"

Fascinated by the differences between China and Sweden, Dalong, who has visited many countries, chose China in the end. Sweden has a population of nine million residing in a land of 500,000 sq km, while the 1.3 billion Chinese live on a land which is about 20 times as large at 960 million sq km. In Sweden the temperature is cool and sometime frigid. China is so vast that it's as cold in its northern part as in Sweden and it's so hot in its southern part that many people there have never seen a single snowflake in their whole life. That's why a big snowfall in 2008 lead to a serious disaster in the south of China. It's so quiet and tranquil in Sweden that some taciturn people in the north have to see a doctor to get treated for "speechlessness". In China, towns and cities, except very remote ones, are always crowded with people, traffic and activity. It is so clamorous that it would be hard to be taciturn. Sweden, a well-developed country, has one of the highest standards of living in the world. China, the biggest developing country, has a very low GDP per person and a lot of problems to tackle, but it is growing at a high speed, and is full of opportunities.

Dalong, like anyone else of his education and experience could easily have landed a good job and a secure and happy life in Sweden, some other European country or North America. However, Dalong is by nature a person fond of challenges. From all his past experiences we can tell that there exist restless genes in his blood that prod him on to adventure. The relatively backward but vigorous China, in striking contrast to Europe and America, was the place he had long been yearning for. "I must have been a Chinese in my previous life," he smiles.

New thinking in PR, Chinese Style

In the early winter of 1994, Dalong returned to Beijing to embark on his chosen career as a businessman. "This was the beginning of my real 'Chinese life'," he says. The first step on the "long march" was to register

a company for importing mini golf equipment. "This was not a great business, but my partner and I survived and could pay ourselves modest salaries," Dalong says. One day he met a friend from a local radio station, and chatted with her about the music. The friend was amazed to learn that so many of the bands popular in China at the time were actually from Sweden. She was also impressed by Dalong's musical knowledge and his idiomatic Chinese. It would be a big waste for such a musical connoisseur and China expert not to be a radio DJ, the friend thought. So she earnestly invited Dalong to her radio station as DJ for a program which was to become a huge hit, syndicated to 15 cities around China: *Scandinavian Journey*. After a few months, Beijing TV called to inquire about Johan hosting a similar show for television, "Music Makers". Dalong's programs opened a new vista for Chinese music lovers, and brought a new kind of European music for them to appreciate.

Engels once said that music is meaningless to the ear that does not cherish it and gourmet food is tasteless to the tongue that does not appreciate it. Dalong is clearly a man of wide-ranging tastes. The musical programs led to more than eight years of weekly programs on Chinese television stations. Together with his wife at the time, local TV host Linlin, he produced a program teaching Western cuisine. I remember taking a great interest in seeing him prepare this "exotic" food while providing interesting digressions on cultural knowledge like how to use knives and forks, and how to toast in different languages. The cooking show attracted a large audience of amateur gourmets—even people with "tasteless tongues" would watch the show for its entertainment value. The accompanying book "Western Food Serves Chinese Tastes" quickly became popular.

"Talent, like pregnancy", goes the Chinese saying, "will give itself away sooner or later". Dalong had now been discovered by local media. From then on this young Swede has frequently appeared as a guest on TV and radio programs, discussing management or politics on one show, singing Swedish folk songs on another.

What TV and radio audiences didn't know is that behind his media career he was successfully building several businesses. In parallel to the mini golf business, he started a record company employing three people, which launched some 30 CDs and arranged several nationwide tours for Western artists. "It was a lot of fun, but not a great business," Johan smiles. "Because of regulations and piracy, we barely broke even, and I didn't even pay myself a salary from this company." He also set up a PR company which was later to be renamed Eastwei Relations, while working as a consultant for Electrolux China, being responsible for local corporate communications. Eastwei was to become the most successful venture; it was soon so busy that Johan had to close the golf equipment company and sell the record company. It was effortless for him to switch from the media sector to the PR industry, according to Dalong, "Maybe I had established a certain reputation as a TV host, so people often asked me to introduce media contacts or arrange simple events like opening ceremonies or product launches. I thought this might be a good business opportunity."

Eastwei grew rapidly. After a couple of years of trial and error, Dalong set about systematically analyzing the future direction of the company. He interviewed some 70 clients, PR managers from the Fortune-500 companies, in order to get the right positioning for Eastwei. Most of these interviewees, he found, categorized PR companies into two general groups: international and domestic. International PR agencies, according to the clients, were professional and had strategic capabilities but often came across as arrogant and

sometimes did not provide strategic advice that was actually relevant to the reality of China. Domestic ones, on the other hand, had no concept of strategy. But they acted quickly, provided good services and had close relations with the media. None of these PR agencies had a clear market positioning, though each had its own features. Dalong said, "A clear positioning is very important for any business. Take cars for example: Volvo implies safety; Mercedes stands for a comfortable ride; and BMW connotes the joy of driving. Customers will choose a brand based on their preferences. The same goes for a business-to-business consultancy like a PR agency: without a proper market positioning, it is difficult to get a competitive advantage. This often leads to price wars."

Dalong also interviewed more than 100 journalists to understand how they viewed PR professionals. One senior chief editor made a particularly deep impression: "I really don't like PR agencies. They just transfer the press releases of their clients to the media, and charge high service fees in the process."

From these interviews, Dalong drew an important conclusion: PR agencies had little understanding of the business of their clients, which made it difficult to provide strategic advice that was really relevant; neither did they understand the needs of local media, what they were looking for and could write about: "We decided that Eastwei should be positioned as a 'knowledge-driven communications company'," he said. "By founding the company on the concept of in-depth understanding and knowledge transfer, we would give journalists the chance to know our clients better. This in turn would allow them to be able to write more in-depth reports that would better serve the business interests of the clients. This was a huge success, internally and externally, and is the kind of knowledge-driven media relations Eastwei has advocated ever since."

Dalong emphasized that "communication is not just about 'newspaper coverage' or 'flashy events'—it is a strategic business function for companies." He would ask his employees to conduct field studies in his client companies in order to know their needs better. "Eastwei PR consultants for IKEA had to wear IKEA uniforms and work as salespersons at IKEA stores for at least two weeks before they were qualified to provide advice to the client."

It is not by chance that Dalong mentions IKEA. The company chose Eastwei as its PR agency shortly after entering the Chinese market. "They weren't happy with the service they were receiving from their initial agency," Dalong says. "I first met all the executives and many store employees to get some basic knowledge of IKEA's advantages in the furniture market as well as its plans for China. We then interviewed a group of journalists. Only after all this groundwork was done did we start working on the strategy. Today, this is common practice, but in those days nobody thought like that—they just proposed some fancy ideas for a launch." Basing activities on consumer and journalist insight has allowed Eastwei to generate many fun and creative ideas for IKEA in China. One memorable press conference for the Complete Bedroom concept was held with the country manager in his pajamas and reporters reclining on IKEA bedroom furniture while watching the Power-Point presentation projected on the ceiling. Reporters in China often suffer from information fatigue, but IKEA has always managed to catch a high level of media attention. Nowadays, IKEA has become a household name, even a symbol of the good life, in China.

A PR event Eastwei organized for Electrolux received a great response from viewers as well. The first buyer of an Electrolux fridge would have the

purchase delivered to his door personally by Waldner, the ping-pong legend. The smiling, blue-clad Swedish table tennis star, loved and revered in China, rode a tricycle to deliver the fridge. It was an amusing scene that was widely picked up by Chinese newspapers and TV stations.

Over the last four years, Eastwei's business volume has increased by an annual average of 50%. Besides its Beijing office, it has set up branches in Shanghai, Guangzhou and Chengdu, with a total of more than 120 employees. From its origins as an upstart, Eastwei has outgrown many of its international and local competitors to become a market leader. "At the beginning, most of Eastwei's clients were well-known international enterprises, like IKEA and Electrolux, which are very good at high-end marketing strategies. It is imperative for them to have a high-end PR agency in China. That's why they have chosen Eastwei," Dalong said. "As our reputation has grown, Eastwei has attracted other giants like SONY, Procter & Gamble and GM as ongoing retainer clients. But as China's economy continues to liberalize, many Chinese enterprises are also becoming aware of the importance of brand image. They have started to break away from the simple pursuit of advertising and started to pay attention to building up their brands using more sophisticated tools. There's no doubt that it's a good choice for them to have Eastwei as their high-end strategic PR partner. I believe it will become the best China's PR agency in future."

The still low level of China's PR industry as a whole has a big bearing on the low popularity of many Chinese national brands. "First, China's PR industry is still immature, and enterprises can't find qualified PR partners," as Dalong put it. "Secondly, it is outmoded, because PR clients are buttoned-down, and PR agencies are stereotyped and lacking originality. An excellent creative idea must be chosen so that it actually supports the positioning and image of the product to be promoted."

Part of Dalong's success seems to be his generosity in sharing his creativity and experience with others. His book *PR, Chinese Style*, which came off the press in July 2006, received a strong and quick response from the whole Chinese PR industry. It was reprinted within only six months. An edition in traditional Chinese characters was released by a Taiwanese publisher in September 2007. The preface was written by Zheng Yannong, vice-president. The endorsements on the book cover read like a *Who's Who* of the Chinese PR industry, featuring heavyweights like Li Daoyu, president of the China International PR Association (CIPRA) and former ambassador to the US, as well as well-known journalists and corporate PR Managers ranging from Coca-Cola and Sony to Airbus and Motorola. One endorsement states that "at last, here is an original PR book that is written for the Chinese market reality." It goes without saying that the book is recognized as a pioneering work in China's PR industry.

The book illustrates a more general aspect of Dalong's business style: doing things differently from his competitors. "While most Chinese agencies focus on the traditional notion of *guanxi* or 'connections first,' we emphasize 'knowledge first.' When other agencies are competing for "clients", we focus our marketing on attracting 'talents'."

Many PR workers said they were "enlightened" when the problems that had long beset them were "cleared up" by Dalong. That's why some people felt that he had "reinvented" China's PR industry. Dalong, distinguishing the subtle nuance in Chinese, understood that the saying was positive but still felt it was too flattering: "We just wanted to attract attention and arouse dis-

cussion, not 'reinvent' anything. The purpose of the book was to summarize and share with readers the best practices of colleagues, clients and competitors. We didn't invent any theory. It was an internal thing for us PR workers. Of course, with the book I want to attract to our agency talented people who are ambitious and enthusiastic and who share our values. As a result, lots of young Chinese and foreign people apply for work or internships at Eastwei. Sometimes they don't even ask for a salary; they just want to learn."

"Actually, it is easy to run a PR agency," Dalong continues. "First, you have to think of your clients, never neglecting their interest for short-term profit. Second, foster a culture where employees do not just passively do what clients ask them to. The agency needs to try to bring their initiative into full play. It should offer employees all possible opportunities, and make them feel a part of it and willing to work hard. Almost every week senior Eastwei consultants will get phone calls from headhunters, often offering much higher salaries. It would be natural for them to 'job-hop' if Eastwei couldn't offer them good opportunities and a pleasant working environment. But they do not easily move once they have been integrated into the Eastwei culture. Third, the agency should have a clear-cut market positioning. Today in China there are too many PR companies that are very much the same. To distinguish ours from the rest we have to have a distinct positioning and uniqueness. At the very beginning we tried hard to canvas clients, make profits and keep the company going. Now we understand it is talent, not clients, which matters in competition. That was the biggest turning point for us. The whole PR industry in China lacks experienced professionals. Under such circumstances, agencies like Eastwei with qualified consultants are becoming hard to find. So in terms of company management, PR agencies in an environment like

Speaking with fervor and assurance at a seminar on PR techniques.

this need to focus strategy on how to absorb and keep qualified professionals, not on competing for clients. On the contrary, we are very cautious in choosing clients, because they are no longer a source of income only, but a factor in deciding our orientation, service offering, and so on."

Eastwei's office is quite different in layout from those of most agencies. Instead of the common one-cubicle-per-person arrangement, six computer desks are put together to form a big oblong table, with the staff sitting face to face across it. There are no separate offices for management; Dalong sits together with his other colleagues in line with what might in China be called "maintaining close ties with the masses". Sometimes, people gather for informal group discussions, but actually each person is occupied with his or her own business. This kind of arrangement seems helpful to natural collegial exchanges and contributes to strengthening team spirit.

The office is filled with luxuriant green potted plants and active young people. The boundary-less office seems to reflect the company's limitless prospects. A corner has been partitioned off as a reception and break room for employees. This is where Dalong sits with me for the interview. An assistant comes in with a tray of cookies and fruit, and I politely decline in the traditional Chinese way. But I would never have imagined that this was not a special treat for the guest—it was the daily "afternoon tea" served to all the staff. At 3 or 4 in the afternoon, everybody stops what they are doing to relax a bit and chat with colleagues over some cookies and fruit. This is really pretty novel to me.

"What kind of boss do you have? Gentle or stern?" I purposely asked some employees. "Gentle", they answered without hesitation. "Will he get mad if you guys make a mistake?" "Never. He will guide you to solutions if you have problems. He always bears his employees in mind. He would rather give up a new client than hurt an employee. To him employees are always the most important." This was really surprising and moving to me. Most Chinese people cherish the belief that "a gentleman is ready to die for his friends." Who would hold back their efforts and talents from working hard for such a charismatic boss with warm human feelings? Headhunters will find it very hard to do anything in Eastwei.

As Eastwei's business continues to expand, Dalong is branching out into new business areas. When clients expressed growing needs for event management services with a communications angle, Dalong and his colleagues set up a new company to undertake these large functions. The born organizer and front-runner, who acted as an auctioneer even in his first grade year, probably will write another book "How to Organize Large Functions" before long. Who knows?

The Swedish dragon takes part in China's rise

Dalong is optimistic about China's development prospects, and confident about his business here. He has spent the prime of his life in this country, and contributed greatly to East-West economic and cultural exchanges. He has been consecutively reelected vice-chairman of the Swedish Chamber of Commerce in China since 1998. During this period he also took the position as the treasurer of the EU Chamber of Commerce in China for two years. He is a successful businessman and a hard-working intellectual. His efforts and accomplishments have been spoken of highly and unanimously by Chinese and foreigners. He will continue to work diligently, with his "next-step" plans on his agenda, and putting his mind again on doing two things or even more at a time.

During his decade or so in China, Dalong has found "more and more foreigners have become fascinated with the country." To help them better understand it, he has given speeches in Sweden on China's culture and social life. His book *I Mittens Rike*, on China's history and culture received a warm response in Scandinavia. But, not satisfied with such a limited audience, he is translating it to English to let more readers know China better.

He also knows the difficulties foreigners come across in studying Chinese. His book *Learn to Write Chinese Characters*, published by Yale University Press, has received wide recognition. Therefore, he has conceived an idea of setting up an educational website for teaching foreigners Chinese. "With the experience of learning the language as a foreigner myself, maybe I

Looking like a true Beijinger.

could do better than Chinese teachers," he said.

Working 13 or 14 hours a day, his energy and vitality seem limitless. He has been busy running a company, hosting TV programs, writing books, giving speeches, setting up websites, and so on. What drives him? "I am taking part in the rise of a big country!" he says proudly.

He still exerts himself to study his beloved Chinese culture. He has recently been reading *The Collection of Classical Prose*, a compilation of essays written over 1,000 years ago in esoteric classical Chinese. In order to do better business in southern China, he is studying Cantonese. He has reached a pretty respectable level of Chinese calligraphy. The autograph in the copy of *PR, Chinese Style* that he gave me looks delicate and graceful, better than the calligraphy of most modern Chinese. The signature, written with an elegant flourish of a dragon flying in the sky, is in the traditional Chinese form. That kind of handwriting is definitely beyond the skills of today's Chinese college students.

He is gratified with his work and life now. He is very good at adjusting the tempo of life. He goes swimming and weightlifting several times a week to keep himself in good shape, though his "swimming style is not very professional," in his own words. Sometimes he strolls in Ditan Park, or goes browsing in an IKEA store. "A visit to IKEA is like coming home. It is in pure Swedish style, no different from that in Stockholm. And the Swedish food there is the most authentic of all in Beijing."

Dalong loves Beijing. "Beijing is my home, though Stockholm is my home too. But they bring me different feelings," he says. "Stockholm is my mother, the city I grew up with; Beijing is my wife who accompanies me and makes me mature. Who can say which one I should love more?" He wants to live permanently in China, and wants his parents to enjoy family happiness in Beijing.

He came to the country because of curiosity about another culture. He found Beijing "makes people feel the rhythm of a huge market of limitless potential." He likes the city's openness and curiosity: "Beijing gives a warm reception to new things as well as newcomers, whether foreigners or people from other parts of the country." This is the place where he started his career and made his business prosperous. But the dragon soaring in the sky will not forget its starting point, where it comes from. "I know my foreign appearance prevents me from becoming Chinese. But I want to work hard to be an honorary citizen of Beijing one day."

In fact, Chinese people long since started regarding him not just as an honorary, but as a true Beijing citizen. .

By Lu Yang
Translated by Yang Yaohua

Personal File

Name: Yano Koji

Nationality: Japanese

Occupation: Actor

Time in China: 7 years

Brilliant As Sunshine

The name Yano Koji may not be well known to the majority of the Chinese people. But when they see his photo they recognize him as the young Japanese who plays Japanese roles in many Chinese movies and TV dramas. In close contact with this handsome and cheerful young man, you will find he is not only a character actor of versatility, but modest and amicable, like a well-behaved big boy next door.

*H*e has achieved great popularity in China, particularly in a period when Sino-Japanese ties have seen flip-flops between warmness and coldness. You will get thousands of results if you look for Yano Koji on any web search engine. His "Yano Koji Bar" in the area of "Japanese and Korean

Stars" on Baidu Website has a high click ratio. His blog *Brilliant with Sunshine* in Chinese has a substantial readership. All of these illustrate the great fame he has attained in this country.

He was chosen by *Newsweek Japan* as one of the "Top 100 Japanese the World Respects", among "adventurers opening up a new world". They are celebrated Japanese

figures respected worldwide for their outstanding achievements. Among them are business tycoons, movie stars, writers and athletes.

From The Ring to Towards the Republic

Yano has just finished shooting a sitcom in Northeast China, and has to fly back to Japan for another movie. And after that he will rush to Yunnan Province to make a TV drama. So I have to interview him in the short time before he goes back to Japan.

Yano was waiting for me in the corner of a quiet café with his assistant. A good place for us! Here the interview wouldn't be interrupted by his fans asking for autographs. I was affected by his typical Japanese modesty and courtesy while shaking hands with him. He was wearing a sweet smile that is familiar to his Chinese audience. On the screen he is versatile, sometimes playing decent and informal roles, sometimes perplexed and arrogant, sometimes friendly and affectionate, and sometimes even wicked and ferocious. He is a typical character actor. Once off the screen, however, he shows his natural quality of being humble and considerate.

Yano was born into an Osaka family of typical office clerks in 1973. Usually in Japan boys are given names with numerals indicating the order in which they were born. But Koji, meaning "Vast second", is not the second son of the family as many think. "My original name is Kouji, not Koji," he tells me. "My friends here told me 'Kouji' sounds very much like the word for 'mouse' in Chinese. So I changed it to Koji. I have three elder sisters. Actually I am the fourth child in the family. My eldest sister is over 40 years old."

"As the youngest and the only boy of the family, you must have been pampered a lot."

"Not at all. My father was very strict with me. That was why I always wanted to run away from home, and go far away from it, when I reached the rebellious age."

He worked as a hotel bartender after he left high school at age 19. "A customer advised me to go to Tokyo and become an actor," Yano said. "So I quit my bartending job, left Osaka and joined Tokyo's Sun Music." With well-defined facial features and a well-balanced slim figure of five feet eight, Yano has the perfect physical conditions for a performing artist.

His road to stardom was by no means a smooth one. The first role he played was that of a corpse, with no lines and not even a facial expression. After that he played a young ruffian, a policeman, and many other minor roles. He always acted these roles earnestly, big or small, and greatly improved his acting skills. "You can learn something even if you play the part of a dead man," he said.

Recalling his life in those early days, Yano explained, "My earnings were meager. The room the company rented for me was so tiny that I could only sleep on the floor. No kitchen. No bathroom. I had to use public restrooms. My monthly salary was only equivalent to about US$300, which is hardly enough to live on in Tokyo."

Yano got a lucky break when he was recommended for a part in Huayi Brothers' TV drama *Eternal Lovers*. Of the five major performers, Yano was the only foreigner; the others were celebrated Chinese artists. It was his first visit to China, and he did not speak Chinese at all. His first experience of China gave him "very fond" memories. "In China, you feel pretty happy and

relaxed in movie shooting. That first experience was really unforgettable. In Tokyo the interpersonal ties are not as close, and you are always under pressure. It is not easy to make friends with your working partners. But here in China, the other members of the cast and crew soon become very close friends." And Yano himself had already made an impact on the minds of Chinese TV drama fans: The passionate Kawashima, the Japanese man he played in *Eternal Lovers* has become an exotic idol for Chinese youth.

In 2001, Yano decided to return to China. He studied Chinese at the Beijing Foreign Languages University. "I was living near Chaoyang Park at that time," he explained. "It took me one hour to get to school by bus. I would spend half a day at school attending classes, and then go back home to do homework and watch TV. I wanted to learn Chinese by watching TV, but it was completely beyond my understanding. One thing that moved me was

Yano in *Proof of Memories*.

the readiness of my Chinese friends to buy me meals, knowing that I had hardly enough money to feed myself. Later, when I started to earn a good salary playing movie roles, I paid them back."

A turn in his fortunes came when he was cast as the Meiji emperor of Japan in the TV drama *Towards the Republic*. He related how eight months after he came to China, Chi Xiaoning, the photographer, called him to say that a TV drama was being shot in Beijing's Daguanyuan Park, and they would need a few Japanese actors. "I rushed over there immediately, and Chi introduced me to Director Zhang Lin."

His role playing the Japanese emperor attracted the attention not only of Chinese media and entertainment circles but also made him a celebrity in Japan as well. This made Yano realize that he could contribute to Sino-Japanese friendship.

From Osaka to Zaozhuang

Proof of Memories brought Yano even greater fame. He played two roles in it—those of Chief Inspector Okada and his grandson Aoyama Yohei. He displayed in the role of Okada a man of complex emotions caught up in the war. This was a far cry from the usual Chinese stereotype of Japanese soldiers, who were depicted as merciless killing machines, cruel and barbarous.

The process of acting is a process of learning, too, Yano found out. Japanese people of sixty or older know the history of the Second World War. They understand that Japanese militarism brought tremendous disasters to the Chinese people. But young and middle-aged Japanese are mostly unaware

Yano in *Proof of Memories*.

of this dark part of their history. Yano admitted that he was surprised when he read the materials and saw photos that director Yang Yang gave him to familiarize himself with that period.

Yano liked the script, because he thought Okada was a genuine figure and not a caricature of the Japanese. *Proof of Memories* won the best product prize of the Flying Apsaras Award in 2005, and Yano then went on to become a contracted actor with Yang Yang's Beijing Golden Pond Movie & TV Cultural Company.

Yano's big achievement is that he has changed the image that most Chinese had of the Japanese as "devil soldiers", and enabled movies about the Japanese invasion of China to be re-shot and watched with a sense of historical reality.

Yano in *Broadsword*.

Yano gave excellent performances in more than a dozen retaken movies like *Little Soldier Zhangga*, *The Clock is Ticking* and *Zhang Boling*.

In retaking *Struggles in An Ancient City* and *Steel Meets Fire*, old movies first shot several decades ago, Yano played villains like Tada and Mouri. To avoid weary repetitions of the two characters, he assumed that Mouri, a Japanese character in *Steel Meets Fire*, was from Japan's Kansai region, and so he did the lines with a Kansai accent.

When *The Railway Guerrillas* was shot in Shandong's Zaozhuang area, the cast and crew had to put up with many hardships in that wild region. Yano stuck together with his Chinese colleagues through thick and thin, making not a single complaint. They felt great admiration for his professional ethics, and on his birthday they presented him with a cake with a picture of a locomotive on it, part of the logo for the movie, and the words "Osaka— Zaozhuang". This symbolized his journey from his hometown of Osaka all the way to Zaozhuang.

Many movie fans are fond of Yano. They like him because of his persistent pursuit of performance skills and his dedication to his profession. They like him also because of his modest and easy-going attitude towards people. "He is not pompous, never thinking he's a star," his colleagues say. They admire him because he, as a Japanese, is bold enough to squarely face the history of the war of resistance against Japanese aggression. He has his own understanding of war and peace.

However, his broad-minded attitude has brought him a certain amount of enmity in Japan. Before the debut of *Proof of Memories*, Yano told media reporters, many of whom were Japanese, that he hoped this TV drama would promote Sino-Japanese exchanges and would be broadcast in Japan. But the media reports of this in Japan were not at all favorable. He received threats, and was once even assaulted in the street.

Nevertheless, Japanese public opinion is warming to Yano and his message. On May 3, 2007, during China Week in Japan, the *Tokyo Shimbun*, one of Japan's four major dailies, devoted a full page to an interview with Yano, under the headline "For friendship, I will go on performing." In 2008, the Mainichi Broadcasting System spent two days with Yano covering his activities in Beijing.

From a "Chinese doctor" to a "Japanese attorney"

Yano has played a dozen roles as Japanese soldiers in the same Japanese

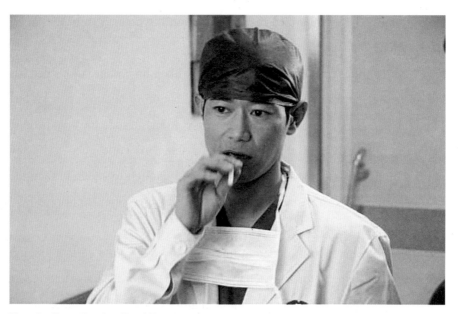

Yano in *Every Day's a Good Day.*

Yano in *My Sun*.

army uniforms. He has tried hard to make these roles differ from each other, and to give his audience a new, pleasing experience each time. To his gratification, the Chinese viewers have highly commended his efforts and have a very clear line of judgment between the player's morality and his performing arts. That is to say, the audience could make an accurate historical evaluation of the crimes committed by the "devil soldiers" and at the same time fully affirm his performing skills in these dramas.

However, Yano was not satisfied with this. He believed that he had met "a bottleneck" in his performing career, and become typecast as a Japanese soldier of the invasion days. He yearned to play the part of a Chinese, and at last his wish came true in 2007, when he was invited to

Northeast China to act the part of a Chinese orthopedist in the sitcom *Every Day's a Good Day*. In the series, the orthopedist falls in unrequited love with the orthopedic hospital director, acted by Wang Ji, a leading Chinese actress. The great amount of dialogue between the two was a real test for Yano's Chinese language, but he rose to the challenge magnificently.

Yano speaks highly of Wang Ji: "I learned a lot, both about acting and social behavior, from her."

It is common in sitcoms for the script to be modified time and again during the shooting process, and Yano would have to abandon the lines he had struggled so hard to memorize the day before. He considered that the biggest challenge for him in his new venture.

As a guest in "Cheerful Chat", a show aired by Hunan TV Station.

Before *Every Day's a Good Day* Yano acted in the TV drama *My Sun*, as a Japanese medical teacher working in China. In *Pursuing His Dream*, another TV drama, he played a star sprinter, and again he moved away from his detested villain roles.

A few days after the interview, he was to fly back to Japan to star in a movie called *A Vagabond*, directed by leading Japanese film maker Kuriyama Tomio. In *A Vagabond*, Yano was to play the role of an idealistic attorney. He said that, having studied the role, he had been attracted by the thought of becoming involved in social issues.

From a "devil soldier" to a "respected Japanese"

At the beginning of 2008, when south China was battered by severe snow storms, Yano appeared on a charity show for disaster relief. "Love has no boundaries," he exclaimed. "We will overcome the difficulties no matter how great they are so long as we are united as one."

As part of his show business career, Yano has been taking singing lessons, and plans to issue a music album co-produced with two Chinese singers. He also intends to publish a book, called *Living*, dealing with his experiences in China.

With all these activities, Yano has had to give up some of his hobbies— mountaineering, horse riding and baseball. But, keen on boxing, he has a punchbag at home, and practices a few punches from time to time.

Yano regards China as his "second homeland", and plans to live and work here permanently. He also wants to buy a house in Beijing. "At present I don't have the financial muscle to do so. The prices are too high and my income is too small," he said. Yano revealed to me that his next goal was to marry a Chinese girl and lead the life of an ordinary Chinese.

By Lu Yang

Translated by Yang Yaohua

Personal File

Name: Luc Bendza

Chinese Name: Ben Zha

Nationality: Gabonese

Occupation: President of Gabon *Wushu*
Association, actor, Chinese
culture promoter

Time in China: 25 years

Dream of Being a Kung Fu Master

Luc Bendza was born into a prominent family in Gabon. But he didn't coast along on the family's fame and wealth, and he didn't follow his father's footsteps as a diplomat or a government official. Instead, he journeyed all the way to the Shaolin Temple, the holy land of Kung Fu in China. There he lived a very simple life together with the Buddhist monks. During his two decades in the country, he has gone through all kinds of setbacks and hardships but has never given up.

I like the way Luc Bendza laughs. It is hearty and affecting. He would always cheer friends up with his laughter. Only children would laugh in that innocent, inattentive way; only the great heroes depicted in novels would laugh that unconstrained, generous laugh.

At 5'7", Bendza has a well trimmed figure of 70 kg. Though not burly, he is strong and vigorous, a muscular and robust figure. As a Kung Fu guru, he never flaunts his skills, just like "still water running deep". Through all the years being engaged in studying Chinese, *wushu* and cultural exchanges, Bendza has built a reputation in China's martial arts and showbiz circles.

A boy wanted to "fly"

There have been quite a number of news reports on Bendza, with different versions of his age. When I asked him about this, he told me that he was definitely born in 1969. "But someone said you were born in 1973?" I asked. "They just want to make me younger," he said, "And I am not unhappy with that." Laughter followed, making all those present tickled pink.

So let's start our story from the very beginning. Born in 1969 in the

Bendza with his mother at the Great Wall.

Republic of Gabon, Bendza is a descendant of a well-known clan. His parents are ranking government officials. His mother is a cabinet minister, and he is the fifth of ten children. His mother, not only having brought up ten children, has carved out a great career for herself, occupying an important government position. This would be unimaginable even in China, where women are said to "hold up half the sky".

Bendza said, "Mom announced at a family meeting that she would back whoever wanted to go to school and support whoever wanted to work. But everybody should cook for themselves if they wanted to eat and make money for themselves if they wanted to spend money. For anyone who wanted to go abroad, there was one precondition: You must be among the top six in the exam scores at school, or stay at home if you are not."

Bendza's grades must have been up to standard, since he was allowed to come to China. "My grades in geology and history were all right, and my grades in maths and physics were average," he said. "But my grades as a whole were not so bad, and I got a place among the top six. Otherwise how could I come to China?" From his grades at school, I can tell Bendza is a person who has a sensitive "first signal system" as described in psychology. He has a quick brain in terms of images and is apt at imitating. Maybe that's why he has handled with great ease the difficulties of learning Kung Fu and foreign languages.

He made good friends with a Chinese interpreter working in Gabon when he was young. This friendship altered his life path. From the interpreter he learned many things about China. He also learned some Chinese songs and a few Kung Fu movements. He watched many movies featuring Chinese Kung Fu. Little Bendza was completely fascinated by these Kung Fu masters with their fighting skills and their *Qing Gong* (lit. light body skills), an ability to jump high and across roofs with flitting motions as if flying. Maybe because his father is an army general, Bendza has a military spirit.

He dreamed of being a Kung Fu master like Bruce Lee or Jackie Chan. Teenagers are full of dreams. Bendza's dreams were always associated with Kung Fu. Now that he got a place in the first top six at school and was then qualified to go abroad as his mother had promised, Bendza asked her for permission to learn Kung Fu in China. But both his mother and father were against the idea of him going so far away and learning something that would not enable him to be a breadwinner?

Maybe he was in the stage of rebellious adolescence, or maybe he was too eager to be a Kung Fu master. The more his parents opposed his idea, the more determined he became. Fortunately, his uncle was the Gabonese ambassador to China, and so Bendza's parents reluctantly agreed to let him come to

China, at the age of only 14, in 1983.

The youngster practicing the horse-riding stance

Soon after he arrived in China, Bendza realized that *qing gong* was not a knack of "flitting in the air" as he had come to expect. Kung Fu masters were just stronger and more vigorous than ordinary people. This realization enabled him to adopt a down-to-earth attitude to learning *wushu*.

With the help of his uncle, Bendza went to the Shaolin Temple. Young Bendza seethed with excitement while watching in person the spectacular performances put on by the fighting monks. He felt the great impact of the Chinese martial arts. He came to understand how hard it would be to master Kung Fu, but he decided to stay and start to learn Chinese martial arts from the very beginning: starting with the horse-riding stance.

The horse-riding stance is a method of training in meditation and for

building up strength, stamina, and potential. It is also used to improve reaction ability. It seems simple, but it's very hard to practice. Beginners find that only a few minutes of this results in them being bathed in sweat and with trembling legs. Old hands can stay in the posture for several hours. When you practice long enough to stand rock-firm on strong legs nobody will be able to knock you down in combat.

At the Shaolin Temple beginners practice the horse-riding stance over an arrangement of sharp nails. "There is nothing hard for me now after several years of that sort of practice," Bendza said. During the years that followed, whenever Bendza encountered setbacks and difficulties, he would always recall what his master, De Shui, told him: "You should hold on straight to the very last minute when you are about to give up."

Bendza didn't speak Chinese when he first came to Shaolin. Without oral communication, he had to imitate others when learning the basic martial arts movements. "I would do whatever the others did," he told me. "I didn't feel it was torture, because I loved it."

The Shaolin Temple provides only vegetarian meals—steamed buns, rice porridge and greens for the three meals every day, and sometime just buns and boiled water. He practiced hard, and experienced severe fatigue. But he loved Kung Fu so dearly that he cared nothing about the loneliness, Spartan life, plain food and hard, monotonous practice. "Life is short," he said, "*Wushu* has kept me sound in body and mind. With good mental and physical health, I have been able to do many of the things I wanted to do."

Eventually, Bendza realized that he had to overcome the language barrier if he wanted to probe deeply into the essence of Chinese *wushu*. At that time, there were no teachers in the Shaolin Temple to teach him Chinese,

so he decided to leave the temple for a while, and go to school to learn Chinese.

Hard-working foreign student

Bendza enrolled at the Beijing Foreign Languages and Cultures University in Beijing, majoring in Chinese. Professor Song was in charge of students from African countries, taking care of everything from day-to-day life to study. Professor Ma Yuming was his teacher of the Chinese language. Ma, a very responsible and experienced professor, could get new students to speak the language in the short period of three months. "Teachers at that time were so strict that you couldn't cut class," Bendza said. "Our teacher would come to look for you in your dorm if you skipped a class."

Bendza made great progress in learning Chinese. He speaks and reads Chinese without a hitch, but still feels a bit ashamed of his poor handwriting. He found it was more difficult for him to write Chinese characters than to learn Kung Fu forms. His bachelor's and master's essays were printed-out computer versions to gloss over his blemishes, since his Chinese handwriting wasn't the best.

He studied English when he was young. Because he exerted great efforts in learning the language, so he has no difficulty when he communicates with others in English. "Many of my school fellows thought English was of not much use and didn't study hard. But when they grew up and went to the outside world, they found English used everywhere. 'If you don't exert yourself in youth,' as a Chinese saying goes, 'you will regret it in old age'. That's very true." He said. With French as his mother tongue, he can switch freely

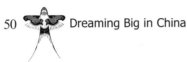

among the three languages. And that has benefited him a lot in his learning and promoting Chinese *wushu*.

After he overcame the language hurdle, Bendza started to study *wushu* at the Beijing Sports University in 1986. With basic training at the Shaolin Temple and his physical robustness, Bendza didn't feel it hard to learn *wushu*. But he clearly understood that there was a wealth of talent in *wushu* circles. Many of these master hands started practicing *wushu* at a very early age. Bendza decided to concentrate on some obscure but very practical Kung Fu skills.

Bendza recalled the first time he saw an expert practicing the subtle-demon staff. He immediately asked Wang Huafeng, a master of this technique at Beijing Sports University, to teach him.

Bendza learned within only one year every technique of the subdue-

demon staff. Wang highly praised the student's earnest and hardworking attitude, and his love for traditional Chinese *wushu*. Bendza then decided to learn the two special skills of Professor Lin Boyuan—*Miao Dao*, or sprout saber, and *Bian Gan*, or short cudgel.

Miao Dao, 1.5-meter-long, is much longer than the normal broadsword, and therefore harder to manipulate. Because it is difficult to handle *Miao Dao*, few people practice it, and even fewer are outstanding. "There are no more than five people in the whole country who are good at *Miao Dao*," Bendza told me.

Bian Gan, a short cudgel once prevalent in China's northwest, is easy to carry and useful for self-defense. Bendza has mastered some practical skills using the *Bian Gan*.

Besides combat skills, Bendza also pays attention to Kung Fu skills for keeping fit. He learned Taijiquan, or shadow boxing, from Professor Men Huifang. He is of the opinion that *wushu* is more of a kind of philosophy than a fighting skill. It provides a methodology for observing the world, he says. *Wushu* practitioners are cultivated to be pliable, tough and firm. They treat all things under the sun with a placid attitude, and gradually reach an internal equilibrium. "*Wushu* makes you understand yourself better, bringing into full play the potential that has been neglected," he told me. "It also helps you solve all the problems you encounter in your everyday life in a placid and balanced way. I have benefited a lot from it." Besides, "Taijiquan is a kind of high-tech art that is absolutely good for one's body and mind. It should be made available to everyone," he suggested.

Bendza found that during the time at the university he also learned from *wushu* a lot of other things that have helped cultivate himself spiritually. His world outlook has changed a lot, and his mind has been broadened. His attitude is now more placid. Friends have noticed that Bendza has become more optimistic, more courageous, more generous and more warmhearted. He offers help whenever his friends are in need. "We should have a sea-like bosom and character," he says. "The sea surges forward, and never stops rolling on in endless waves. There will be inevitable frustrations and difficulties in our life. But there is nothing too hard to overcome so long as we adopt a sea-like attitude."

Many Kung Fu masters adhere to the traditional habit of furtively testing their apprentices. Bendza has a very deep understanding of Chinese culture, and he always gets praise from his teachers. Once a teacher gave him an assignment and left, saying, "Get practicing!" It was in the depth of winter. He kept practicing in the snow until all his fingers were numb with

cold. After long hours the teacher came back. He commended Bendza in his mind, though he said nothing to the student. From then on, the teacher passed on to Bendza all his skills with all his heart. The teacher just wanted to know if you had the perseverance, the willpower and the respect for *wushu* and for the teacher. Some foreign students asked Bendza why some teachers just assigned practice, and didn't teach them anything else. "You don't understand," Bendza said, "The teachers are testing you to see if you are eager and sincere."

After seven years of practicing *wushu* in China, Bendza took part in the First Shaolin Martial Arts Festival, and his excellent *Miao Dao* performance won him the golden medal. He has won the same title seven years running. That was why his colleagues say, "Here comes the champion!" every time he appears. The mayor of the organizing city of Zhengzhou spoke highly of the young black man, and the two have become close friends. In many other world *wushu* tournaments that followed, he also received high marks in boxing, sword, *Bian Gan* and all-around contest. And even back home in Gabon the president highly commended him for his achievements.

When he was still a student at Beijing Sports University, Bendza was dispatched by the International *Wushu* Federation to France, Spain, Demark, Zaire and South Africa as a *wushu* instructor and umpire.

He is deeply impressed by the charms of Chinese *wushu*, and hopes very much to spread it the world over. "*Wushu* comes from China, but belongs to the world," he said.

In 1991 Bendza discussed with the Gabonese Minister of Sports the possibility of setting up a *wushu* association in that country. However, although Karate and Taekwondo were popular there, nobody seemed interested in Kung Fu, even though Bendza explained that the former two martial arts also have their roots in Chinese culture.

Thereupon, Bendza started to offer short training courses when he was on home vacations. During the 15 years from 1991 to 2006, Bendza traveled to and fro between Gabon and China numerous times. The Gabonese Ministry of Sports finally gave him the go-ahead in 2006, and Bendza was entrusted with the selection of members for Gabon's first national *wushu* team. In 2007, the one-year old team, led by Bendza, took part in the 9th International *Wushu* Tournament and the Huangshan Traditional *Wushu* Invitational Tournament, both held in China.

During this period, the Chinese *Wushu* Association gave Bendza tremendous support. Every two years, he would come to Hebei *Wushu* Center with a group of Gabonese youths for training, and get prepared for the next international *wushu* tournament. Chinese tutors would teach them all-round skills,

almost everything from Nan Quan, sword and staff to Taijiquan. In addition to having his team trained in China, Bendza invited Chinese teachers to go to Gabon to train his team.

"It is of great benefit for these kids to learn *wushu*," he observed. "They regard *wushu* practicing as a form of recreation. Interest is the best teacher, and many youths have been turned away from the path of delinquency by *wushu*. Indeed, many parents are eager for their children to learn it.

Like a hardworking farmer tilling the land, Bendza spreads *wushu* "seeds" in Africa. As a technical officer and a world-class umpire of the International *Wushu* Federation, Bendza, is "longing for the day when *wushu* spreads to the whole world." He said, "All people, whether they are from

Bendza with Kung Fu stars Jackie Chan, Frankie Chan, Liang Xiaolong, Steven Chow, and Yu Hai.

In *Charging Out Amazon.*

developed or developing countries, can benefit from *wushu* in building up their health, fully tap their potential, vigorously conduct their careers, and make more contributions to their own countries and to the whole world."

A Kung Fu master of showbiz

In China, it is seemingly a regular pattern that Kung Fu gurus end up in showbiz. With his foreign appearance, Bendza certainly brings an exotic flavor to the Chinese movies and television dramas he performs in.

Bendza came to the attention of Hong Kong movie circles when he won a gold medal at the Second Shaolin *Wushu* Tournament in 1992. Since then, he has starred alongside Kung Fu greats like Jackie Chan.

He appeared in *Kung Fu Kid*, *Replacement Killer*, *Shaolin Dragon* and

others. But his proudest performance was in *Charging Out Amazon*, which won the highest prized bestowed by China's Ministry of Culture.

In 2007, Cui Yongyuan, a leading TV anchor produced a series titled *Grand Spring Festival Gala*. There were five leading actors, including Cui himself. Bendza played the role of Da Zhu, a comic figure. Well aware of his fluent Chinese and Kung Fu skills, Cui created the role tailor made for him.

In recent years, Bendza has been increasing his emphasis on international cultural exchanges. In order to promote Chinese *wushu* culture further, as well as improve the prospects for Chinese showbiz, he has been talking with foreign companies about promoting the movie *Kung Fu Kid* on the world market.

With his standing in world *wushu* circles, his close ties with the showbiz industry and his ability to speak three languages, Bendza is a natural promoter of international cultural exchanges. Being generous and chivalrous by

With Cui Yongyuan, an anchor of China's Central TV Station.

Bendza finally meets his idol Bruce Lee in Seattle, USA.

nature, characteristics typical of Kung Fu practitioners, he is well known for being ready to help others, whether friends or strangers.

His wife is a typical northern Chinese lady, cheerful and lively. Having majored in fashion design at college, Mrs. Bendza runs a clothes boutique.

Bendza regards China as his second homeland. Since he came here, he has grown from a teenager into a *wushu* master, a movie star, an expert on cultural exchanges, a successful businessman, world *wushu* federation official and the chairman of the Gabonese *Wushu* Association. He has experienced exciting changes in China. And, most important of all, he has realized his childhood Kung Fu dreams here. He feels he has grown up together with China.

By Lu Yang

Translated by Yang Yaohua

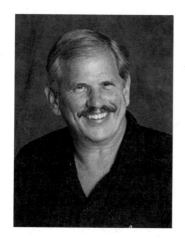

Personal File

Name: Daniel J.Dudek

Chinese name: Du Dande

Nationality: American

Occupation: Economist

Time in China: 1 year

A Foreign Model Worker Protecting Our Homeland

Daniel J.Dudek, chief economist of the Environmental Defense Fund of the United States, is a cheerful and humorous man who loves nature and is dedicated to his work. In his quest to protect the earth, he flies around the world like a migratory bird, engaging in environmental advocacy. His dream is to make this world one suitable for mankind.

$\mathcal{W}$hen I met him, Mr. Dudek said, "I hope my wife will read your article, so that she will know how excellent her husband is." His Chinese colleagues all laughed.

The chief economist of Environmental Defense once served as President George W. Bush's environmental adviser and worked with ecologist Dr. Abel Aganbegyan, who was known in Russia as the "Father of Reform". He has worked with many statesmen, officials and scholars in promoting his ideas on ecological preservation. His suggestions have been noted by many leading political figures such as former British Prime Minister Tony Blair, China's former Premier Li Peng, China's current premier Wen Jiabao and former and current directors of China's Ministry of Environmental Protection. In recent years he has made great contributions to China's environmental protection, and was given the Friendship Award by the Chinese government. This is the highest honor a foreign expert can receive in China. Dr. Dudek has been an advisor to many public and private agencies in many countries. These agencies include the OECD, Polish Ministry of the Environment; United Nations Conference on Trade and Development; Regional Environmental Centre, Budapest; US Environmental Protection Agency; Chicago Board of Trade;

US Department of Energy's Advisory Board; British Petroleum Company; Massachusetts Institute of Technology; Ministry of Environmental Protection of the People's Republic of China; and many other agencies. He has published more than 100 essays and articles on market-based environmental policies.

He regularly flies around the world, especially between China and the United States, in his quest to protect our environment.

How Earth Day determined the path he would take

This ruddy-faced, well-built man is five feet ten inches tall and weighs 175 pounds. He served in the army, which is why today, despite being in his 60s, he remains energetic and exuberant. When discussing his age, he referred to the Chinese zodiac, saying, "I am a pig" (born in a Year of the Pig by the traditional Chinese calendar).

Daniel J. Dudek was born in a small town in Massachusetts in 1947, to parents of Polish and German extraction.

The town was host to a unique tradition: Every year, it would host a meeting at which citizens would work on local development issues. His father's side of the family was Polish, but his father was born in the United States. His grandparents lived to very old ages. As a teenager during the Great Depression, his father dropped out of school to earn money to feed the family. His mother came from a poor German family, and her father was a blue-collar worker. His father was a signalman in the US Navy in the Pacific during World War II and he met his future wife during training, and they married after the war ended. It was in such a blue-collar, small town, tricultural context that Daniel came of age. Perhaps such an upbringing laid the foundations for him to become a cosmopolitan environmental protection expert.

He confesses that he is envious of children today, who enjoy such amenities as electronic books and high-tech gadgets. Much of his own younger years were spent growing potatoes and tomatoes, and this led him to develop an understanding of the harmony between mankind and the world of Nature. His mother taught her children about bird watching and read *Silent Spring* to them, a pioneering work which planted seeds of ecological awareness in their young minds. From this book, Daniel learned about how changes in the environment are reflected by the migration patterns of certain bird species. Today,

Watching birds with his father and two daughters.

he continues to feed birds and spends winters looking forward to the return of migrating birds in the springtime. Every year, he is eager to see which birds return to his feeder.

Daniel also shares another connection with birds—one linked to his position at Environmental Defense. Environmental Defense grew from a small organization into a major global player in the field of ecological protection when scientists discovered DDT had caused reproductive failure in ospreys, a fish-eating bird, on Long Island, leading to a worldwide movement, in which Environmental Defense was heavily involved, to stop the use of the chemical weed killer.

Daniel believes his life as a teenager and young adult was rather conventional—studying hard, attending college, serving in the army. The only unique part was a period during which he got very little sleep, because he had to work in a factory while studying. While such hardship was known to few of his fellow students, it helped him develop a stronger will and greater sense of perseverance.

He jokingly said, "I am still a young man. I can quickly bury myself in my work at any place in spite of jet lag brought by my frequent flights around the world."

He served in the army in South Korea in 1967, and was honorably discharged in 1970. Before April 22, 1970, Daniel J. Dudek had no clear plan for his future after he returned to New York.

However, everything changed for him on the first Earth Day.

He still has a copy of the *New York Times* published on April 22, 1970, in which the main headline announced the inauguration of Earth Day. He said, "Although I had just returned from Korea, I knew the first Earth Day was meaningful. I was impressed by Koreans' awareness of recycling, and at that time I thought it might change some part of the world." As he stood among the crowds who had taken to the streets in celebration, the young man decided the path he would take in life.

In 1972 he graduated from Massachusetts University with a bachelor's degree, and in 1975 he completed his master's degree in agricultural economics at the Davis Campus of the University of California. He remained at Davis until he finished his doctoral degree in agricultural economics in 1979.

"I think my passion for environmental protection has a connection with what America was doing and China has also succeeded at—manned space flight," he said. "The first picture taken from outer space showed us a blue planet with a beautiful environment and oceans. I was deeply touched by the picture, and felt that the earth really is our common homeland. The ecological system created by Nature—the most valuable wealth Nature gives us—shouldn't be harmed by human activities. That is to say, every citizen of the world, no matter what part of the world he or she comes from and in whichever country he or she lives, should make a due contribution to the protection of our common homeland."

Protecting our common homeland has become Daniel's commitment to the planet.

From 1975 to 1982, Daniel worked at the Economic Research Service of the US Department of Agriculture as an agricultural economist. His work there focused on understanding the water quality problems stemming from irrigation farming practices. From 1982 to 1986, he taught at the Agricultural and Resource Economics Department of the University of Massachusetts, and studied the problem of acid rain.

In 1985 he was promoted to professor, teaching environmental economics. One day, he received a phone call. The caller asked if he would be interested in joining the non-governmental organization Environmental Defense Fund. At that time, it was a small organization, with only one economist. After that call, he faced a fork in the road: "Continue grading students' papers and teaching what has happened or trying something new?"

He explained, "I had worked in universities for many years. Although my suggestions on policies were reasonable, they were not easy to communicate to the media or policy makers, or to implement." He believed the Environmental Defense Fund could become an ideal platform from which he could realize his dream.

The Environmental Defense Fund is today a renowned non-governmental and non-profit environmental protection organization with one of the longest histories among such groups. Its current membership stands at more than 600,000. Since its founding in 1967, it has remained committed to developing new approaches to economic, scientific and legal strategies in developing the most innovative, fair and economically pragmatic methods of addressing the most urgent challenges mankind faces. Daniel became a leading activist within the group, and in 2002 he became its chief economist.

How a market method broke the acid rain deadlock

Daniel is very proud of his decision. "After I joined the Environmental Defense Fund, my first job was to affiliate with the American delegation for the negotiation of the Montreal Protocol. This convention was about how to control CFCs and other chemicals harmful to the ozone layer," he said. "I developed a market-based policy to control CFCs—i.e., to allow some countries to reduce CFC emissions, while allowing other countries to increase CFC emissions, which would limit emissions globally and eliminate industry's objections to the cost."

It was a long and hard period of negotiations. All industrial figures indicated that compulsory control of fluorocarbon pollution would slow industrial development and cause economic depression. However, by the time the debate had begun, researchers had discovered the hole in the ozone layer over Antarctica, and were beginning to understand the severity of the problem. This had a dramatic impact on the negotiations, and media all over the world began reporting on the issues surrounding the hole in the ozone layer and how pollution threatened the planet. This put pressure on negotiators, forcing them to reach an agreement on the issue.

To Daniel's regret, however, his market-based solution was not included in the final agreement. Because the idea had not been tested, people were uncertain of its effectiveness.

During the US presidential campaign in 1988, neither the Democrats nor the Republicans dared ignore environmental protection. However, their levels of support for, and understanding of, environmental policies were very different. So Daniel and his colleagues decided to work out a plan upon which both parties could agree. They called their method Project 88. One tenet of the plan was to use emissions trading to address the issue of acid rain. Capitalizing on presidential campaigns and using them to resolve environmental issues could be called a typical American approach. When George Bush Sr. won the election, Daniel, the chief executive officer of the Environmental Defense Fund and a lawyer were invited to the White House to discuss how

Bush could become the environmental president he had promised he would be.

When the authorities approved the use of emissions trading to address the acid rain issue, the impact was tremendous. The Environmental Defense Fund had struggled to find a solution to the problem of acid rain for 16 years, and now there was new hope on the horizon. In the previous years, scientists determined the severity of problems, and media and NGOs informed the public about the problems, but the government would say, "The problem is difficult to address, and we need more research," and then some research budgets would be created. But the process normally ended at the conclusion of the research. This had been the case for the previous eight years, so when Daniel's team visited the White House, they were unsure of the situation they were dealing with. They were surprised when the executive department told them: "Let's start working on this." As Daniel put it: "It was the beginning of a six-month period beyond imagination. During that time, I was at the White House nearly every week, and often for several days in a row, and we jointly developed the plan for emissions trading with the executive department."

Daniel and his team tried to develop environmental resource markets worldwide to reduce and control emissions of atmospheric pollutants from both stationary and mobile sources. President Bush praised their work, saying it had rescued the acid rain issue from deadlock.

Daniel participated in market development of the sulfur dioxide allowance trading system, which the US implemented to reduce acid rain. He also worked with other programs. These included reshaping CFCs' tradable manufacturing rights to meet the requirements of the Montreal Convention; strategies approved by the Environmental Protection Agency (EPA) on the trade of hydrocarbon and nitrogen oxide emissions from mobile and stationary sources that were carried out in areas where air quality didn't meet national standards; and programs dealing with the management of volatile organic compounds in Illinois, as well as regional nitrogen oxide emissions in the eastern US, and greenhouse gases globally.

The work that Daniel and his team initiated is of great importance to the US and the world. The scope of their work extended beyond the United States, leading to the development of Poland's first pollution emissions trading scheme; the first international greenhouse gas trade; the first swap in pollutants involving sulfur dioxide and carbon dioxide between two companies with different obligations, different pollutant positions, and different locations on opposite sides of the US; and the development of the world's first in-company greenhouse gas trading system within the British Petroleum Company (BP).

Daniel committed himself to promoting emissions trading, which is based upon setting a firm limit or cap for the total emissions of power plants and factories. It stipulates that such facilities can either keep any emission allowances below their limit for future use or sell them to companies unable to meet government emission requirements. This approach is called "total amount control emissions trading".

One of the milestones of Daniel's many years of hard work was the inclusion of emissions trading in the 1997 Kyoto Protocol, which seeks to limit global greenhouse gas emissions and control climate change.

Bringing American experience to China

In 1990, the United States amended its Clean Air Act, and established emissions trading as the policy tool by which SO_2 emissions, the chief cause

Visiting a power plant.

of acid rain, would be controlled. Implementing regulations were developed by the US Environmental Protection Agency in consultation with the Acid Rain Advisory Committee, of which Daniel was a member. The goal of the program was to cut total US sulfur dioxide emissions by 50% from 1980 levels by the year 2000. Emission sources would have to begin controlling their emissions by 1995, but trading began earlier than this. It was also designed to significantly reduce the cost of achieving the same environmental benefits. This new policy development in the US caught the attention of the Chinese government and its environmental departments.

At that time, China's 1.3 billion people were facing great environmental challenges, and pollution's negative impact, stemming from the burgeoning of Chinese industry. The government did not have tight controls over pollutants that cause acid rain. However, China's policy at that time was to fine those who exceeded pollution emission limits. For example, under the Pollution Levy System in 1995, power plants emitting SO_2 above the discharge standard were charged 200,000 yuan ($31,000) at maximum. However, controlling emissions through the use of control technology such as flue gas desulphurization costs several billions yuan. As a result, it has been cheaper to pay the pollution levy than to control emissions, so the system ultimately proved ineffective.

Wise men learn from others' mistakes. Realizing the necessity of drawing upon foreign experience, the Ministry of Environmental Protection recruited foreign experts to study experimental approaches, which were then in their fledgling stages. The government was laying the foundations for the adoption of a fusion of foreign and Chinese methodology to develop a market-based environment protection strategy. It was particularly interested in Daniel's acid rain control strategy, and invited him to give lectures in China. His first task was to provide policy suggestions, such as developing economic approaches to pollution-control measures. It was Daniel's first trip to the country, and would be one of many.

Daniel became more than a lecturer. Having introduced emissions trading in the country, he proved the effectiveness of the scheme step-by-step through a series of demonstration projects. In 1999, the Environmental Defense Fund began its official partnership with China's Ministry of Environmental Protection. Then-Premier Zhu Rongji developed an agreement with US Vice-president Al Gore to conduct a bilateral project on using emissions trading to address the acid rain problem in China. Since

the organization had been conducting pilot projects in Liaoning and Jiangsu provinces, the Ministry asked the EDF to contribute its experience from these projects to the bilateral international effort. The project was concluded in 2001 with a favorable review both by the Ministry of Environmental Protection and the US Environmental Protection Agency. However, this was a very small-scale effort, and a much larger set of experiments was needed. In 2002, the MEP issued an administrative regulation which was the beginning of the project which came to be known as "4+3+1". This project involved Jiangsu, Shandong, Henan and Shanxi provinces; Shanghai, Tianjin and Liuzhou cities; and the Huaneng Company. The project tested specific guidelines for the critical elements of SO_2 emissions trading.

"The results from China's population and pollution control are amazing," Daniel said. "Remember, this is a huge country and has a tremendous impact on all aspects of the global environment and economy. The Environmental Defense Fund highlights the use of science, the economy and a market-oriented approach to work out a reasonable and sustainable solution to problems, which is very unique to this organization. This approach has already proved to be feasible in China."

He went on, "In June 2004 our cooperative projects were examined and approved by the Ministry of Environmental Protection of the People's Republic of China. Personally, I feel satisfied with what we have achieved, not only because of the great amount of practical work we have completed, but also because in the course of our cooperation Chinese officials, experts and other colleagues have come to understand and have gained awareness of the differences between the applications of a good policy in two different cultural systems, and thus we could infuse Chinese characteristics into our designs and practices."

Speaking with determination, he said: "We should never forget that it took America 20 years to propose, discuss, legislate and implement this policy, while in China it was already approved by the State Council in December 2005. If the concept is realized in the 11th Five-Year Plan and is well observed, it will take far less time for China to achieve this specific policy's development and implementation than it took for America to do so."

Since the market-based policy of SO_2 emissions trading seemed to be catching on, Daniel and his colleagues in the Beijing office turned their attention to the underpinnings of this policy. Close inspection of the fundamental environmental laws in China revealed that the failure to obey the law was not punished severely enough. In fact, fines were limited to amounts far lower than what it would cost to control pollution. Together with the MEP's Bureau of Environmental Enforcement and Supervision, the EDF began a project to analyze the issues surrounding the legal cap on penalties. Specifically, they wanted to know how much benefit a company would enjoy from not complying with the law or regulations. If companies did not have to spend money to control their pollution, those funds would be available for other business purposes. To assess this benefit, they adapted to Chinese circumstances a computer model used by the US EPA in the determination of civil penalties. This Chinese model and training in its use were made available to local environmental standards enforcement officials, who applied it to cases within their jurisdictions. The findings were shared with the Natural Resources and Environment Committee of the National People's Congress.

How the American expert became a foreign model worker

For Daniel's outstanding contribution to China's environmental protection, the Chinese government in 2004 bestowed on him the National Friendship Award, which is the highest honor a foreigner can win. He was also received by the leadership of the Communist Party of China on several occasions. At the friendship prize award ceremony in the Great Hall of the People he was selected as the representative of the prizewinners. He was deeply touched by being honored as a foreign model worker. "I felt very surprised at the time, because I didn't expect I would win the award, or that it would even be given to someone from the field of environmental protection, as the

Receiving the Friendship Award certificate in September 2004.

latter hadn't been given much attention prior to that. It gave me a great sense of responsibility, because the award wasn't just honoring me but also my thousands of colleagues working on environmental protection, including both Chinese and foreign experts," he said.

Daniel added, "I have been working on environmental protection for more than 30 years, and that was the highest award I have received. It was definitely very surprising and stimulating. But I believe that rather than glorifying me, it's symbolic of the fact that in its quest to produce an affluent society, the Chinese government is paying increasing attention to environmental protection and people working in this field. It has led to a great leap forward in people's environmental awareness."

On the day of the award ceremony, the winners were invited to the 2004 National Day Reception. Daniel seized his toast with Premier Wen Jiabao as an opportunity to advocate his idea of using a market-based approach to environmental protection, which Wen very much appreciated. As they clinked glasses, Wen said that a key strand in China's construction of an affluent society was environmental protection, and this would be a theme well embodied in the country's 11th Five-Year Plan.

Daniel always stresses the relationship between mankind and Nature when meeting Chinese leaders. He once told both Chairman Hu Jintao and Premier Wen that the relationship between man and Nature was very important to China's construction of a harmonious and environmentally friendly society. He said that the ecological balance could be upset, because while the planet could clear out some of the pollution, mankind's impact could become too powerful and overwhelming. The consequences of such damage, which is inflicted every day in the pursuit of development all around the world,

could be more disastrous than the threat of nuclear, chemical or biological weapon attacks precisely because pollution is unleashed every day. Economic development in the US has been harmful to the earth, and that damage has come about as a result of the extensiveness and speed of the growth of the economy. However, the US has learned from that damage and built effective environmental management systems. China's rapid development has also had serious environmental consequences for which the goal of creating an environmentally friendly society is an antidote. That is to say that while undertaking the task of development people must monitor fluctuations in the environment as seriously as they pay attention to changes in their bank balances.

Daniel was relieved to find that the Chinese leadership heeded his words of warning.

Chinese leaders have consistently stressed the country's determination to pursue reform and opening up, and that China will never weaken in either its will or its determination to construct an eco-friendly society. The improvement in Chinese environmental consciousness can be seen in the fact that the Beijing Olympics were hosted under three themes: Green Olympics, People's Olympics and Hi-tech Olympics.

In March 2005, Daniel was appointed director of the foreign members of the CCICED Task Force on Environmental Governance. In June 2007, he was appointed by the Chinese government as one of the 23 foreign members of the CCICED, the top consultative body dealing with China's environment and sustainable development. The Chinese government hopes this foreign model worker can come up with more and even better ideas in the future.

A Chinese addition to a happy family

Behind every successful man, there is a great woman. We wanted to know about the great woman behind Daniel and the story of their romance.

After leaving the army, he lived in, what is for America an old farmhouse which was built in 1790. His neighbor was an elderly woman originally from New York City, and despite their age difference, the two got along well and became close friends. The old woman spoke highly of Daniel and took it upon herself to help the young man find a bride. She asked everyone—her friends, her friends' friends, her friends' friends' friends—to introduce Daniel to a girl. She would tell people: "I know an excellent young man. Please introduce him to a good woman."

According to Chinese folklore, the Old Matchmaker arranges marriages between young men and women. It seems his American contemporary is also a kind old woman. Daniel's neighbor's efforts finally succeeded, and Daniel met an excellent young woman, who already ran two restaurants.

Daniel tried to win her heart through her stomach, and invited her, the restaurant owner, to taste some of his amateur cooking. It was like teaching a fish to swim. The fare he served her was substandard, but he sang as he toiled in the kitchen. However, she was taken with his charm and praised every dish he served and appeared to really enjoy the meal.

After that, it was her turn to satisfy Daniel's appetite. Every day, the restaurant's chef would telephone him to ask him what he wanted to eat. "It turns you into a king if you marry a woman who own a restaurant," he said.

With his beloved.

The two married and moved to upstate New York, where they bought a farm. They were ready to have a baby and enjoy their happy day. His wife quit running the restaurant to become a homemaker. They adopted a relationship based on traditional roles, in which the man was responsible for outdoor duties and the woman for indoor duties, including childcare. According to Daniel: "It is not right to entrust the nursery with your kids. Their first teachers should be their parents, who greatly influence them. Of course, in America, it's hard to manage your job and family simultaneously, but I'm lucky. I have the opportunity to choose my career and have a good job. If we have a child, the grandparents can help with childcare duties, and that will be good for the child's development."

However, things didn't go as expected. The couple found they were unable to have a child. Daniel tried again and again to comfort his sorrowful wife but did so in vain. But they found the answer to their dilemma when Daniel's wife joined him on a business trip to Jiangsu Province. They saw

A happy family.

many parents pushing baby carriages along the streets, and nestled inside were lovely babies with beautiful faces. Upon seeing these adorable infants, Daniel's wife proposed to her husband adoption as an option for them to start a family.

Daniel smiled: "To adopt a child is more difficult than to have our own, because the adoption agency we went through is very responsible. It insisted on knowing the details of our lives, education and economic status. It gave us information about the children up for adoption. It is a long, expensive journey and a responsible deed. In this way, I got a lovely daughter, and two years later, another one from Changzhou joined our family." He pulled out photographs of his daughters from his wallet, and showed them to me. Then he produced another one of his wife, smiling and holding the youngest daughter as she curiously studied the camera lens pointed at her. "It was taken when

we adopted our youngest daughter," he explained. Today, they are aged ten and six.

Like most fathers, Daniel is close to his daughters. He taught them important lessons, and they worshiped their wise father. He took particular joy in the girls' affection. When they were young, they would often demand: "Dad, give me a hug." Of course Daniel would comply. When they were a little older, they would still ask: "Dad, can you put me to bed?" The father remained zealous in his work, despite the fact that he was older and not as strong as he had been in earlier years. He remembered receiving a phone call during one of his business trips to China. On the other end of the phone was his wife, who said the eldest daughter told her: "Mom, I miss dad very much." Daniel was deeply touched by her sweetness. "I have no idea what she will be like in her teens," he said. I told him the Chinese saying: "Daughters are parents' warm clothes for when it's cold." He was happy to hear this.

Daniel very much admires the profundity of Chinese culture, especially its ancient understanding of the importance of harmony between mankind and Nature, as expressed in the Chinese phrase *"tian ren he yi"* (harmony between mankind and Nature). From the first day he set his foot in China, "environmental protection" and "China" became two of the most frequently used words in his vocabulary. He believes the connection and love he has for China has been greatly strengthened by the adoption of his two daughters. Daniel hopes that they will not forget their Chinese roots.

The Chinese additions to the family, the two girls' laughter, brought great joy and fun to the family—so much so that the couple "couldn't remember life without them". The parents wanted their daughters to learn Chinese in case they wanted to work in China when they grew up, but the eldest daughter would come home from her lessons, saying: "Too hard. It is unbelievably hard." The girls had left China at such young ages and then were immersed in American culture and the English language. Fortunately, their school had some Chinese teachers able to convey Chinese culture, making it easier for the girls to learn Chinese. The family observes some Chinese traditions; they make dumpling around Spring Festival, buy Chinese clothes and the children have read *Journey to the West*. Daniel hoped they will not forget their roots.

The two children have many interests, which their parents support to help the children develop to their full potential. The eldest daughter first took lessons in gymnastics, then moved on to golf, tennis, swimming and computers. At age 4 and a half, the youngest daughter requested piano lessons, so

Enjoying nature and love.

Life is so colorful with daughters around!

the elder sister also asked to take them. But she wasn't attentive to her study of the instrument and instead, takes greater interest in horseback riding and hopes to someday have her own horse. She likes football, and the younger sister has subse-quently also developed an interest in the sport. The two influence each other. The girls are very energetic and exhaust their parents, so that they rarely enjoy sufficient sleep. However, Daniel believes caring for such lively kids would help the couple remain happy and busy, and also keeps them young at heart.

"I have only one hope for them: to live a happy life. It is easy but hard. Some people can easily find happiness, while others can't. I hope my daugh-ters could tap their potential, and live and work happily, and turn our planet into a beautiful homeland."

Daniel planned on bringing his daughters to China during the Beijing Olympic Games. They were going to spend their first week appreciating the Olympics, the second week traveling including visiting their birthplace, Changzhou.

Since adopting his two Chinese daughters, Daniel has felt a greater sense of responsibility. He said, "They are gifts from God. As a father, I am responsible for not only the two of them but also for the environment."

By Lu Yang

Translated by Zhang Ruiqing

Personal File

Name: Dominic Johnson-Hill

Chinese Name: Jiang Senhai

Nationality: British

Occupation: Shop owner

Time in China: 15 years

Creative "Plastered 8" with Its Chic T-shirts

Kung Pao Chicken; second-hand drugs; Socialism is good; Women can be heroes. These are all stuff that couldn't be more familiar to Beijing natives. But they are neither fish, flesh nor fowl if you put them together. But when a couple of years ago a *lao wai* (foreigner) printed them on T-shirts they have grown into a fashion among young Chinese and foreigners alike, just like the "I Heart NY" T-shirts in New York City. He is Dominic Johnson-Hill, or Jiang Senhai.

*J*iang Senhai, a lanky Briton from London, is in his thirties, but friends call him "Lao Jiang" or Old Jiang. He speaks fluent Mandarin with a typical Beijing accent, and likes very much to say he is a transplant "passing his life in Beijing". To many Chinese friends, he is passing his life here quite well.

Old Jiang enjoys a wide reputation with his store at home and abroad; several major foreign news agencies have told his story; and many fashion magazines have published his photos and stories on prominent pages. Since he has become a well-known figure, his customers and even passers-by on the streets often pick him out in a crowd, and ask him to have a picture taken with them.

Creative T-shirts

To many, "Plastered 8" doesn't make much sense. "Plaster has a three-fold meaning: First, it's an adhesive bandage; second, it means sticking something to walls or T-shirts; third, it means drunk, completely intoxicated'," he explained. "The pronunciation of eight in Chinese is close to that of prosperity, meaning good luck. That is why I picked '8'."

Johnson and his personal-
ized store.

The motifs on his T-shirts bring to all Chinese visitors a knowing smile: three mugs imprinted with "Socialism is good"; "Oppose eating and drinking extravagantly and be frugal"—Mao's highest instruction printed on a 400-gram food stamp; a taxi price sticker announcing ￥1.2/km; a 1921-1971 sign for the 50th anniversary of the Chinese Communist Party.

He takes pictures of such old stuff when he finds them while taking strolls in *hutongs* (typical old Beijing alleys). Old Jiang says he likes taking a walk along these backstreets, where he finds a lot of old relics of Beijing that are novel to him. These patterns, signs and logos, which Beijingers tend to ignore, are charming items in his eyes. He likes stuff from the 1970s the most, not only because they are reminiscent of the past.

A bus stop sign; a subway ticket; a Beijing-brand thermos bottle; an enamel washbowl with goldfish designs; a "Serve the people" sign; a flyer for second-hand drugs with a contact cell phone number—everything has its own interesting background story, and can become inspiration for his creativity.

He explained, "*Kung Pao* Chicken is the Chinese dish most familiar to foreigners. So I designed the motif of *Kung Pao* Chicken for my T-shirts. It's funny and interesting," he added. "The price of taxi flagfalls has gone up from ￥1.2/km to ￥2/km. The palm trees in the picture 'Sunrise in Beijing' are not real ones on a beach, but plastic ones erected by the Beijing government."

The ￥3 subway ticket is his pet design, and has become a bestseller. Now, the price of the ticket is down to ￥2, so the ￥3 ticket has more collection value. The picture of migrant workers with a background of highrises is another of his inspired designs. In order to void copyright infringement, he has altered at least ten percent of the original picture.

Brainstorms

For a time he wore a T-shirt imprinted with the message "Second-hand drugs" plus his own phone number on it. But he soon found himself inundated with phone calls, and so he stopped wearing it.

The T-shirt with the slogan "Serve the people" has proved to be very popular. The slogan is a widely known quotation from Mao Zedong, and the T-shirt design includes a phone number. "The attraction is the idea that you can phone the late chairman and talk with him about serving the people," he explained.

Talking about political

Creative and fantastic T-shirts.

slogans printed on T-shirts nowadays, Old Jiang said he doesn't choose political themes, because politics keeps changing all the time. Furthermore, he has to meet the international demand for his merchandise, and too-political designs do not meet the taste of foreign customers. However, Old Jiang does not shy away from political stuff completely. In his office two blocks away from his home, we found him and his employees busy with a T-shirt design which carried the words "Carrying out revolution by workers, farmers and soldiers" for Reuters newsmen to use during the 2008 Olympic Games. During the 17th National Conference of the Communist Party of China, he worked out a design with the words "Harmonious 17th Conference", also for Reuters. These kinds of T-shirts, he said, are usually custom made, and, if his client gives him the nod, he can sell them on the market.

Display of collectibles

In addition to more than several dozen T-shirt designs in Plastered 8, on display are many other items full of typical English phlegmatic humor. Just outside the door of the store is a spittoon that has a Chinese characters for double happiness on it. "I'm fed up with these people who love to show off with their business cards regardless of time and place, and I throw their cards in the spittoon as soon as they turn around," he explained. Erected in front of the shop window is an imitation bus stop sign with a route indicator that reads, "Bus 88, originating at Terminal Plastered 8 to Terminal Zhongnanhai; Service hours: 10 a.m. to 10 p.m." Funnily enough, it shows several stops along the route. The so-called bus service hours are coincidentally the same as those of the store's business hours. Against the back wall is a range of enameled mugs imprinted with "Beijing 8", "Subway ¥3 ticket", etc.

Created by Old Jiang himself, many T-shirts are sold out within one or two weeks. Some other stores, attracted by Old Jiang's lucrative business, have started to carry T-shirts with similar motifs, like "Women hold up half of the sky," and so on.

While browsing around in Nanluoguxiang Alley, this reporter saw a couple of shops selling similar graphic T-shirts not far from Plastered 8. "I do not resent those people who copy my ideas," Old Jiang told me. "But there are two foreigners who sell exactly the same designs as mine in their store in Beijing's Soho area, like 'Women can be heroes.' I hate such persons." The Peking Opera Master Gai Jiaotian used to say "Those who learn from me will survive; those who copy me will perish", I told him, trying to console him. "Their copies don't look exactly like mine," he said, seemingly feeling better, "They don't have the afflatus. And fortunately so far there is no Chinese copying my designs."

Many other T-shirt store owners and this reporter are quite curious about where on earth he gets his inspiration from. On a rainy morning, sitting face to face with me, Old Jiang told me his story, starting from his very first day in China.

Mysterious China

"I didn't speak any Chinese before I came. At that time China was not fully opened yet to the outside world. I just had had a few meals at some Chinese restaurants in London. That was my knowledge of China at the very most. I didn't go to college. I visited Africa, South America, and India after

middle school. I imagined that in China everybody was clad in the same kind of clothes and everybody was riding a bike." At the beginning of the 1990s, China was still a very mysterious country. "I am eager to go to places that are not easy to get to," he emphasized. At the suggestion of his younger brother, he first visited Qingdao in 1992. To his dismay, nobody was dressed in the Chinese tunic suit, and very few people were riding bicycles. A poster showing a father and a son admiring a thriving factory made him even more disappointed, because Old Jiang doesn't like "factories".

The year next, Old Jiang came to Beijing. In Beijing, he lived a typical foreigner's life: living in an apartment building exclusively for foreigners since he was not allowed to live in the *hutongs* within the Second Ring Road, where Chinese clustered; paying double for air tickets; playing baseball in an embassy compound; having no Chinese friends; and only a few bars available.

Depressed

In 1995, his family transferred a sum of money from the UK to Beijing as a subsidy for him. But he never expected that he would have to wait for two full months to get the money. He went to a Bank of China sub-branch almost everyday, and was told the money hadn't come yet almost everyday. Two months! Old Jiang, now on a very tight budget, got really mad at the bank clerks. Finally he was referred to the head office of the bank in Xidan. There were no computers in the head office and the guy in charge was working among piles of papers, smoking leisurely. After he explained his awkward situation to the bank clerk, Old Jiang received the money the following day.

He had more than enough of these financial embarrassments. So, in 2000 he moved to bustling and flourishing Shanghai. The biggest gain he had in Shanghai was a daughter from a short-lived marriage, and not much cash left in his pocket. Then he took his child to the Philippines, to Australia and then finally the UK.

In 2002, he wound up back in the UK, with only 600 pounds to his name. But, he felt a bit strange at home. Because he didn't have a credit score and didn't pay tax, it was difficult for him even to get a debit card. He had to apply to three banks before he got one. Recalling his experiences in China, he found himself yearning for the life there. In 2003, he found himself back in China again.

He landed his first job at a language training school. Gradually he made more and more Chinese friends. In order to learn the language quickly, he moved to the Big Bell Temple area, and shared an apartment with a Chinese friend. There were not many foreigners living in that area and thus the police easily noticed his relocation. But the police, being acquainted with this foreigner, didn't interfere with it, though the relocation didn't conform to the regulations.

For a period of time, Old Jiang lived in a *hutong* not far from the Yuanming Yuan Park, with many Chinese painters and artists as his neighbors. Later, some of them became really famous and, accordingly, their works got really expensive. "Life would be much easier if I had bought some of their works," Old Jiang joked.

Fond of hutongs

One year later, he moved to Nanluoguxiang Alley, and settled down in a *siheyuan* (traditional Beijing-style courtyard house). He got married here and the couple gave birth to two babies. Everyday, he would either stay with his wife and kids or bat the breeze with neighbors. He is enamored of Chinese-style humor: "Beijingers have a sense of humor similar to that of Britons, a kind of passive humor."

He would ride a bike far and near to shoot pictures of anything he thought interesting. Then he got the idea of making and selling T-shirts with designs displaying the Beijing street culture he had been fascinated with for

Plastered 8

14 years. "Plastered 8" opened for business at the beginning of 2006, with much help from his *hutong* neighbors. In Old Jiang's eyes, the *hutongs* are the soul of Beijing, a living museum, compared with which the Forbidden City is just a place full of foreign visitors and foreign architecture.

"I don't like the idea of turning my Nanluoguxiang Alley into a bar street like the Houhai area," he said. "That's why I have frequently visited my neighborhood committee to persuade to do something meaningful."

He continued, "If we turn our *hutong* into a bar street, it will be finished. The *hutongs* are the soul of Beijing. They are still alive. If we want to show our children the history of Beijing we should give them something original and meaningful, like a *hutong*."

The Committee couldn't fully understand his suggestion for limiting the number of bars in Nanluoguxiang Alley. Houhai Park was very nice before 1999, Old Jiang told them. Now it looks like a KTV scene, a real nightmare. Nanluoguxiang has taken on its shape in a natural way, he pointed out, saying he hoped the local government would display creativeness in developing the *hutong*.

Interacting with the local government

In June 2007, Old Jiang planned his first fashion show, with a catwalk set up in his *hutong*. The neighborhood committee was very happy with the idea. But he forgot to inform the police station of the event until the day before the show. The police told him that he had to apply for a permit. He thought it was too late. The police sent him directly to the East City District Government of Beijing for help. He got tacit approval from it. So the fashion

A vivid and novel ad.

show was held in front of "Plastered 8" on time. The show attracted several hundred viewers, and the police had to come to help with the traffic. It was a great success.

With the experience of his first successful fashion show, he started "Creative Market" together with *Urban Pictorial* magazine. When everything was ready, the neighborhood committee said no to him just a week before the opening, on the ground that there was already a cultural market in Wang-fujing Street not far from there. He canvassed the committee for his plan by attaching the significance of the market to the upcoming Olympic Games. Finally he brought the committee around. The day the market opened, all the committee members came to help. The fashion show, with a catwalk by models, was attended by crowds of people. To his delight, many migrant workers from construction sites came to see the show, too.

He wanted very much to organize a bigger "Creative Market" in 2008. But it was not easy to get a permit for big social functions during the Olympic Games, he was told. He understood that, and postponed it to September, when the games were over. The committee was satisfied with his new plan.

There are about 60 T-shirt motifs in the store. Every year he comes up with about 15 new designs. "The fashion shows in the *hutong* really boost sales," he said proudly.

Great reputation

Old Jiang has been living in China for 15 years, I figured out; almost as long as the time he stayed in Britain. He has become famous, though not rich yet. Passersby often ask him if he is the foreigner on a TV show. He always feels awkward at being identified like that, because he is not the kind of person who likes to be famous.

However, being famous is obviously beneficial to him. Every day he gets phone calls probing the possibility of cooperation with him, or asking him for dealership in other parts of the country. Now Plastered 8 has wholesale businesses in Hunan Province, and Guangzhou and Wuhan cities. Beijing's 798 Art Factory will soon be on the list. A London fashion company has bought his copyright and is ready to promote his merchandise. Orders keep streaming in, and it is hard for him to keep up with demand. The main problem, according to Old Jiang, is that it is not easy to find Chinese garment makers with stable production quality. Seventy percent of the products processed for him are returned because of quality defects. He has been consider-

ing a UK garment maker as the main processor to guarantee quality, though the overhead cost would be doubled.

Recently Old Jiang paid a visit to Shanxi Province, one of the biggest coal producers in China. There he saw many new buildings erected by rich coal mine owners. To him they were ugly, and in stark contrast with those of the poor. He said, "I am going to use this concept in my next design. Some Chinese may not like it."

Business expanding

As his business expands, Old Jiang has hired more workers, and even purchased a special computer program for his inventory. But he has been under pressure lately because the business earnings do not keep up with the ever-increasing expenses. He has three children to feed, he said. They go to decent schools, and decent schools are expensive. Besides, he has some charitable undertakings to carry out with friends.

Old Jiang's first full-time employee was a store assistant hired at the end of 2007. Now the company has seven or eight employees, and he doesn't stay in the store as much as he did before.

Old Jiang likes to give customers discounts when he is at the store. The wholesale price he offers is very low, too. That makes his employees grumble a lot. "Too much profit-seeking is no good," he said. "I even don't have a plan for my business. I just do it while musing about what to do next." T-shirts are still his main line, though he carries some other items like custom-made teapots, ash trays, etc.

Attachment to China

I had my second interview with Old Jiang on May 19, 2008, the first national day of mourning for the Sichuan earthquake victims. "We don't have earthquakes in Britain," he said. "I saw TV coverage of some earthquakes in Turkey. I didn't feel too much worried because I didn't speak the language and didn't understand what had happened too much. Now, this is my home and I understand the language, and, what's more, I have visited the place which suffered the earthquake. These days I am so obsessed about the children still under the ruins that I can't sleep at night." He looked worried, on the verge of tears.

In the days following the earthquake, he and some foreign friends bought clothes, bedding and tents for the victims. His wife, seeing so many baby orphans without milk, bought formula and feeders and delivered them to the quake area by DHL. Asked if he had considered going to the quake-stricken area, he said he had given up on this idea because Chinese people are getting richer these years, and they had donated great amounts to the victims, and the relief work would be hindered if everybody drove out there.

"It's the first time I have seen the Chinese people so united and the whole nation stand up to help. Maybe this has something to do with the socialist system. Capitalism is sort of selfish," he said. "The Olympic Games will certainly increase the cohesion of the Chinese people." This reporter accidentally saw his name on the list of donors posted in his Nanluoguxiang Alley. He smiled when seeing this. To him, that was just something unimpor-

tant and a role he ought play.

In addition to his donations to the earthquake area, he conceived three earthquake-theme designs for T-shirt motifs. The first one shows a Chinese soldier holding a baby in his arms; the second shows a female doctor attending the injured; and the third shows children in the disaster area. The accompanying words on all of them are "We are heroes." He did this in the hope of urging the nation to help the people in the quake-stricken area to rebuild their homes with greater determination and solidarity. People are encouraged to download these designs online, and print them on T-shirts either for self-use or for sale—all free of charge.

Old Jiang told me he would donate all the profits from these T-shirts to the earthquake victims, and help the local people rebuild schools. "We are all

A peaceful courtyard life.

heroes so long as we do our best, no matter how little we can do for them," he said.

Hutong *life*

After escorting his children to the kindergarten every morning, Old Jiang has his breakfast standing in the street. Or like some local folks, he comes out to the street to buy milk in his pyjamas, and then has leisurely chats with his *hutong* neighbors. "Just like a little old man who doesn't want to part from his old dwelling," is how he described himself.

"I often feel like taking a nap at noon, as the Chinese people do. But I would seem very lazy to my employees if I did that. I have to set an example to others, and so just dream of it." In the afternoon or in the evening, he likes very much to have a stroll in the *hutongs* for one hour or two to catch some inspiration for his T-shirt designs. Or sometimes he finds a good restaurant. Different from most foreigners, Old Jiang goes to bed at 9 or 10 o'clock at night.

Unless he has to take business trips to other parts of the country, he stays in downtown Beijing. He doesn't go to places like the Sanlitun bar area, doesn't like the hustle and bustle of life there, and doesn't like to see drunken foreign visitors.

Beijing, in his words, is very masculine, with ugly shoe-box buildings and very wide streets. But he likes the conflicting feeling. The new office building of CCTV, for example, "is very powerful, though it is quite controversial." The old stuff in Beijing is very "indigenous", not modern. But that is the flavor of Beijing. Beijing has accomplished in only 30 years what

Enjoying an ordinary but happy life with his wife and children in Beijing.

Great Britain accomplished in 200 years, he noted. So it is natural that some changes have inadequacies. He said he likes these conflicting factors behind Beijing's rapid urbanization.

The future of his children

His three children are growing up in the *hutong*, and, just as their father does, speak very fluent Chinese. In Beijing, many foreigners have their own social circles, basically isolated from the Chinese people. Their kids go to international schools, they booze with friends in bars at night and don't know much of either their mother country's culture or Chinese culture. The children become "internationalized kids", without a sense of cultural belonging.

Old Jiang's children play with and enjoy delicious food with their

Chinese friends, and sometimes even sleep over at their neighbors' homes. You will never get prosperous if you go alone, and you have to be open-minded about other cultures, Old Jiang added. That's why he urges his children to keep close relations with China and to develop their careers in the country.

As British citizens, it is not easy for the children to go to local Chinese schools. The eldest is already six years old, and goes to a French school; the second goes to kindergarten; the third stays at home with a nanny. Old Jiang wants very much to apply for a "green card" but doesn't know how to. He only knows that a very few well-known foreigners or those who have made great contributions have this special privilege. He doesn't think he belongs to that group. With a Chinese green card, his life and the future of his children would be ensured in the country.

Now, as the Beijing Olympic Games are approaching, Old Jiang is getting busier. He believes a great number of foreigners will come to visit his *hutong*, and many of them will like his Chinese brand T-shirts. He is busy designing T-shirt motifs with Olympic themes for Reuter's journalists in Beijing.

By Shan Jinliang
Translated by Yang Yaohua

Personal File

Name: Belen Cliadra

Nationality: Spanish

Occupation: Translator

Time in China: 4 years

A Spanish Girl and Her Dream
of Traveling in China

At the mere mention of Spain, your ears are likely to ring with the lively tempo of flamenco, as the alluring movements of Hispanic women—coupled with the enchanting image of the matador—appear in your mind's eye. But when you first meet the young Spaniard named Belen, you'd probably never guess that this beautiful girl once translated the play *Teahouse*, written by preeminent Chinese novelist Lao She, and dreams of traveling around China.

Standing before me is a beautiful, elegantly dressed Hispanic girl with celebrity looks, wavy dark-brown hair, enchanting eyes and a delicate figure. As it happens, she is also a Spanish-language expert employed by Xinhua News Agency. Her name is Belen Cliadra.

If I had to decide over again, I'd still choose to study Chinese

Belen grew up in the southern Spanish city of Granada, over 700 km from the capital, Madrid. Granada is a seaside city nestling at the foot of the Sierra Nevada mountain range. From her days as a primary school student right up to her university years, Belen never once left her hometown. While pursuing studies at the University of Granada, her major was English translation. It would seem that neither Belen's geographical location nor the direction of her studies would bear any relation to China. And this may, in fact, have been true—had Belen not selected Chinese as her second language at university.

When I asked Belen why she chose to study Chinese, she was candid in her answer. "In Spain, very few people have attained proficiency in Chinese,

and speaking the language would come in handy when seeking employment. I was also filled with curiosity and a sense of mystery about Chinese characters and the ancient Asian civilizations. It was this combination of factors that led to my decision to study Chinese. You could say it came about by chance."

When Belen first set out to learn Chinese characters, she quickly found it to be an exacting and arduous task. The more she studied the language, however, the more her interest grew, and soon it was as if she had become spellbound. Studying Chinese, she found, enabled her to understand China's rich history and culture. It was this fact, in particular, which fueled and intensified her interest in the language.

As if in the blink of an eye, Belen's four-year university life came to an end. This, in turn, meant that it was time for her foreign-language studies to be wrapped up. Faced with this transition, Belen found herself overcome by a powerful desire: to go to China and continue studying Chinese. She was conscious of the fact that China's doors were wide open, and knew in her heart that she couldn't let them close behind her. With this realization, Belen applied for and received a scholarship from the Spanish government. Without further ado, she packed her luggage and boarded a plane bound for Beijing.

When Belen first arrived in Beijing in the summer of 2004, she made a startling discovery: All of a sudden, she had become a "mute"! Despite having studied Chinese for several years in Spain, Belen found that as soon as she arrived in China, she was literally speechless! The only thing for her to do was to start from scratch. Without delay, Belen immersed herself in Chinese-language studies at Beijing Foreign Studies University (BFSU), putting her nose to the grindstone and studying as assiduously as ever. Gradually, she was able to speak and understand Chinese. In June 2006, Belen completed her undergraduate studies at BFSU, graduating with distinction.

Belen still rejoices over her initial decision to come to China. "If I hadn't come to study in Beijing, I probably would never have learned Chinese," she says. "And, if that were the case, not only would my prior Chinese studies have been for naught, but I'd also have no way to appreciate the artistic charm of the language."

Speaking from the heart, Belen told me that coming to China was a kind of preordained destiny. "I've long had an avid interest in Chinese history and culture," she says. "Since coming to China, I've found myself growing increasingly fond of this country and its people. So while my initial decision to study Chinese was a bit random, I'd definitely make the same choice over again if given the opportunity. For me, it's more than a passion; you could say I'm in love with the Chinese language."

I asked Belen why she wanted to stay in China. "My primary aim in coming here was to learn Chinese," she replies. "Since my major at university was translation, I definitely want to master the language. If I came all the way to China, spent several years here, and was still unable to learn Chinese well, that would have been a complete and utter waste of time."

Belen is extremely dedicated in her pursuit of learning Chinese, and plans to spend another year or two pursuing a master's degree in Chinese-language studies. Her current job in Beijing enables her to consolidate her language skills while saving up some money for tuition. It also affords her time to search for a suitable mentor and specialization so that, in the near future, she can pursue advanced Chinese-language studies at the postgraduate level.

Belen feels that Spain is lacking in its understanding of China. As her

Chinese level improves, Belen plans to introduce more of China to her home-land, translate more works of Chinese literature into Spanish, and foster increased connections between the cultures of these two countries. "Promoting closer relations and enhanced cultural discourse between China and Spain will be extremely meaningful," Belen says.

Weighing every word: Belen's translation of Teahouse

After graduating from BFSU, Belen joined the Spanish-language team of Xinhua News Agency's international bureau, where her main responsi-bilities include translating and polishing news articles. She was overjoyed to accept this position, as it meant she could stay immersed in a Chinese-language environment and continue to improve her fluency in Chinese. In her free time, Belen enjoys reading Chinese novels, play scripts and other literary works. She is also constantly looking for opportunities to use and improve her Chinese.

In 2007, Belen seized one such opportunity—which, for her, could also be considered a challenge. At the suggestion of her former teacher, a profes-sor of sinology at the University of Granada, she teamed up with two other young Spanish friends to translate famous writer Lao She's masterpiece play *Teahouse* into Spanish.

When I asked Belen why she decided to translate *Teahouse*, she cited three reasons. "First, this famous Chinese play was long ago translated into English, French and German—but never into Spanish," she says. "Even though *Teahouse* was written a century ago and depicts life in an even earlier era, traces of that life can still be found in present-day China. Through the play, one can gain a deeper understanding of Chinese culture as well as the personalities of the Chinese people.

"Second, the degree of difficulty presented by this translation project was a good match for me and my co-translators, as young scholars of the Chinese language. It would have been a much harder task, for example, to translate ancient Chinese literature. Third, 2007 marked the centennial of the modern Chinese drama. Completing a Spanish translation of this famous Chinese play was an especially meaningful way for us to mark this anniversary."

For Belen, however, the most important reason was plain and simple: She loves translation! Besides, translating *Teahouse* offered an ideal way for her to continue her Chinese-language studies. By pushing her own limits and, in the process, gaining practical experience in applying the language, Belen was confident that she could further improve her proficiency in Chinese.

Belen decided that she would face this challenge head-on, and do whatever it took to get the job done. The first time she picked up and read the play script, she was completely unfamiliar with the era and life depicted by Lao She—and hadn't the least idea how to get started with the translation. She dug up a dozen reference books relating to the history of the Republic of China, as well as the folk customs of the time, and began to peruse them one by one. After sifting through millions of words of historical records, Belen was able to gain a thorough grasp of Lao She's storyline. She was finally ready to get started on the translation.

The three young Hispanics divided up the translation work for the three-act *Teahouse*; Belen, it was decided, would be responsible for the first act. "I was conscientious and meticulous in my efforts, choosing each word with precision and care," Belen recalls. "After completing the first draft, I went

to work revising, embellishing and retouching the translation. I revised the entire first act at least ten times from beginning to end, and can't even count how many times I went through and edited individual segments of the text. Altogether, it took over three months to finish translating the first act of Lao She's *Teahouse*."

Today, the three Spanish amigos have already finished translating the entire text of *Teahouse*, and the manuscript is now being consolidated and polished by their former professor in Spain. If all goes well, the Spanish version of this famous play will be published in 2008.

"The professor was very pleased with my translation," says Belen. "That gives me a great sense of gratification. I look forward to the day when our Spanish rendition of Lao She's *Teahouse* finally hits the bookstore shelves. On that day, our goal will have been realized!"

Belen also told us that translating *Teahouse* enabled her to gain a deeper understanding of Lao She. "I didn't discover his sense of humor the first time I read *Teahouse*. Only by reading the play over and over again did I gradually appreciate the wit and overtones of humor embedded in his language. With this awareness, I could then seek out corresponding Spanish words and phrases to render a better translation. As one of my university professors once remarked, reading a book doesn't necessarily leave a deep or lasting impression; it's the process of translating the work that leaves the deepest impression."

As Belen eagerly awaits publication of her first work, she's confident about her future as a literary translator. "Despite the fact that I didn't translate *Teahouse* independently," she says, "I'll definitely be able to translate many Chinese literary works on my own in the future."

Belen's words express her infatuation with the literature of China. When she gets talking about the works of several 20th-century Chinese authors—such as Lu Xun, Lao She, Ba Jin, Ding Ling and Su Tong—Belen reveals not only a deep interest but also an abundance of opinions. She relates to me, for instance, that she is fond of Lu Xun's unique style and rigorous use of language, and the deep connotative meaning contained in his novels. "Translating the works of Lu Xun requires tremendous ability," she adds.

Belen also offers her assessment of modern writer Su Tong. "Although he writes mainly short tales depicting everyday affairs, his writing is acute and humorous—evoking images of real life."

As for this up-and-coming translator's next literary "target", Belen is still seeking out and pondering a variety of options. Regardless of the choice she makes, we have every reason to believe that Belen's linguistic skills will continue to improve, and that her translation style will mature with each passing day. In the meantime, we eagerly await Belen's next translation.

Staying in China: a rare and precious opportunity

Despite Belen's youth, she is the first Chinese-fluent native Spanish expert employed by Xinhua News Agency. Her involvement in translating and editing news releases for the international bureau makes her an invaluable asset to the agency.

In order to strengthen the international influence of Chinese news reports, Xinhua's international bureau decided to increase the number of foreign-language analytical news stories and commentaries. In general, world news and editorials written by Xinhua reporters or research fellows with

the Chinese Academy of Social Sciences are selected for translation into the Spanish language. These articles, which are harder to translate than typical news pieces, may number up to three per day. To ensure that her translation is as precise as possible, Belen often matches the original Chinese article against the Spanish translation. Based on her understanding of the Chinese language, she can search for the most appropriate Spanish words or expressions, giving full play to her linguistic advantage. In the event that she is unable to finish translating an article during working hours, she takes the initiative to take the manuscript home to revise and polish.

Belen's colleagues still recall how the workload at Xinhua's Spanish-language department shot up in October 2007 during the 17th National Congress of the Communist Party of China. On October 15, the day of the opening ceremony, congratulatory letters came flooding in from foreign governments; letters not received until noon had to be translated the same day, with the translation volume totaling several thousand words. The department manager called up Belen, who happened to have the day off, and asked whether she could help out with this urgent task. Without the least hesitation, Belen promised to leave immediately for the office. When the manager apologized for having her come in to work on her rest day, she responded by saying, "I'm here to work for you. If overtime is required, it's no problem whatsoever." This tireless work ethic, her colleagues point out, is simply Belen's natural disposition; as long as there is work to be done, she can always be counted on to show up.

Belen's extreme conscientiousness in her work and studies has also left a lasting impression on her Chinese colleagues. Whenever she encounters an unfamiliar Chinese character, she always searches for it online, looks it up in a dictionary, or consults her Chinese coworkers. She brings a scholarly attitude to her work, never performing her duties perfunctorily. As a result, the articles translated or edited by Belen boast a high accuracy rate and are highly praised by her colleagues and superiors. They all agree: If you hand a manuscript to Belen, you can rest assured that she'll do the job well.

During Xinhua's annual renewal of foreign experts' employment contracts, the department leadership unanimously agreed to give Belen the highest raise possible as a reward for her outstanding job performance and achievements.

Although Belen is a foreign employee at Xinhua, she doesn't consider herself a "guest" in any sense, and actively participates in discussions on the selection of news topics and planning of special reports. Once, when an article about an important international conference was being drafted, the department was planning to include the same standard content as usual. Belen, however, suggested that some lighter tidbits could be added to the report—for example, the favorite foods of conference attendees, the hotel at which they stayed, etc. This would make the article lighter and more appealing to readers.

When we ask Belen about her job at Xinhua, she tells us excitedly that she finds her work very interesting. At the news agency, she can quickly learn about major events occurring in countries around the world, and translate articles detailing these events to promptly share them with readers in Spain and other Spanish-speaking countries.

For Belen, another benefit of her job is that she is able to constantly learn new things. "I really like this kind of work style and pace, which entails changes on a daily basis," she says. "I feel that I'm constantly being chal-

lenged. Being able to continuously track important world affairs and developments and reflect them to readers through our articles gives me a strong sense of accomplishment."

Belen also really likes her work team. "My Chinese colleagues are very good to me," she says. "Whenever I have a question, I can always turn to them for answers. With their help, I can rapidly improve my Chinese as well."

Every time Belen's birthday rolls around, the international bureau always sends her a congratulatory letter, and many colleagues wish her a happy birthday in person. When she occasionally falls ill, her colleagues contact nearby medical clinics for her and even personally visit her in hospital.

The kindness and caring that Belen receives from everyone at the office gives her a feeling of warmth and family.

"China is developing so rapidly now," Belen says. "So many things are happening every day, and living and working here is very exciting. China is at a crucial stage of historic development. I'm lucky to be able to come and work in China during this important period. Considering how precious this opportunity is, why wouldn't I want to stay? Some foreigners in China are only here transiently; after working or traveling for a short while, they pack their bags and leave as quickly as they came. As for me, I'm very fond of China and Beijing. Besides, I've become used to life here, and plan to continue living and working in China."

Enjoying the sights and sounds of China

In her free time, Belen enjoys visiting Houhai and the Temple of Heaven, or ambling through the small hutongs dispersed across the city. She also enjoys hanging out in some of Beijing's quieter and more secluded bars and snack shops, where she can chat with friends, grab a bite to eat, and enjoy a few moments of rest and relaxation.

Belen is particularly fond of the Temple of Heaven, situated in southern urban Beijing, where the emperor once performed sacrifices to Heaven. "The Temple of Heaven is close to where I live. It's really quiet there, with ancient trees and an atmosphere that evokes a sense of great transformation. Although Beijing's parks are beautiful, too, and have lots of flowers, there tend to be few trees. Relatively speaking, I prefer big trees, so I often visit the Temple of Heaven on weekends. When the weather is agreeable, I plant myself under a tree for a few hours, and leaf through a book while listening to the old folks in the park singing Beijing opera. The music seems to come

to life through the book's pages, creating a distinctive sound with a lingering charm. It's wonderful."

Peking Opera—the quintessence of Chinese culture—is a traditional art form which is in danger of extinction but is being protected. At some opera theaters, shows are often staged specially for foreigners. In Belen's opinion, these so-called "Beijing Opera" performances are unnatural and laden with overacting. The shows put on by the elderly opera fans, in contrast, are unrestrained and full of zest. Although these park performers may not be professionals, they sing straight from the heart, making their performances interesting and flavorful.

When Belen has a long holiday, she likes to call up some friends and set off to explore China's diverse tourist destinations. During the four years that she has been in China, she's already visited a fair number of regions, including Shanghai, Luoyang, Xi'an, Hong Kong, Chengdu and Kunming. Which place left the deepest impression on Belen? "Lijiang", she replies. "It's beautiful there."

She explained, "I stayed for three or four days on Sifang Street in the ancient town of Lijiang. The town has narrow zigzagging alleyways, a small square, and lots of small shops, as well as coffee shops and restaurants. If you get up bright and early, the streets are very quiet; the freshly washed cobblestone streets are bright and clean, giving you a feeling of comfort and coziness.

"Sometimes I didn't have any purpose in mind, and just wanted to seek out a certain feeling. I could walk through the cobblestone streets, find a coffee shop to sit down in, curl up with a book and spend the better part of the day reading. That was a refreshing feeling."

Belen is particularly fond of small cities and towns, and their serene atmosphere and exquisite charm. "Spain has a lot of ancient cities and towns. Lijiang actually brings to mind an ancient Spanish city called Delado, which I visited when I was a young girl. In this small city, located south of Madrid, there are many small winding alleyways and cobblestone streets; the city's architectural style differs somewhat from that of Lijiang, but the feeling is similar. As soon as I arrived in Lijiang, my childhood memories of Delado

were instantly rekindled. That's the extraordinary power of travel."

Belen feels that, in general, China's large metropolises are basically all the same, and lack clear distinguishing features. She found the Sichuan capital of Chengdu, however, to be an exception. "At the time of my visit, while Beijing was still in the depth of winter, flowers were already blooming in warm and sunny Chengdu. As the sun shone brightly, people gathered in teahouses to engage in light gossip and enjoy a cup of tea. I found the atmosphere truly relaxing. Just like a Chengdu local, I whiled away a few hours in one of the teahouses. It was a real pleasure."

There are still many places in China that Belen dreams of visiting, including the ancient villages around Mount Huangshan in Anhui Province and the expansive regions of Xinjiang and Tibet. "China is so vast, with exquisite natural landscapes to be found in every corner of the country," Belen says. "Traveling around China requires a lot of time. Right now, I'm devoting myself to my work and studies. In the future, there'll be ample time to explore and enjoy China's beautiful scenery."

Life in China isn't easy for a foreigner

Having lived in Beijing for over four years, Belen has had plenty of opportunities to interact with and get to know the people of China and Beijing.

"The biggest difference is that I'm a 'laowai' in China since I have a foreigner's face," Belen says. "This is different from Europe, where it's difficult to judge someone's place of origin based solely on his or her appearance. In general, there's a certain distance between Chinese and foreigners. Chinese

A peddler weighs fruit for Belen.

people tend to be more introverted and reserved, and often have difficulty expressing their feelings. Only when you've known them for some time do they open up to you and become more passionate and friendly. Unlike the Chinese, Spanish people tend to be passionate and open from the start. We can be very close to each other, even if we've only met a short time before."

Despite these differences, Belen has also noticed many similarities between the Chinese and Spanish peoples. For example, both peoples treasure their families to a great extent; and both enjoy the warm and lively atmosphere of get-togethers with friends.

Belen says that she enjoys living in a community filled with Beijing's distinctive flavor. In her neighborhood, she can listen to old folks' small talk and banter, and enjoy a variety of Chinese dishes, including hand-pulled noodles, lamb soup, meatballs braised in brown sauce, and diced chicken

with chili peppers. Her neighbors also treat her very well; the lady living across the hallway even gave her moon cakes during the Mid-Autumn Festival.

Among Belen's most memorable recollections are the embarrassing episodes she experienced when she first came to China, which mostly resulted from her immature language skills. Whenever she went out shopping, for example, shopkeepers often had no clue what she was trying to say. The result was that she frequently made a fool of herself.

Occasionally, Belen has to handle miscellaneous matters on her own, such as a leaking toilet or a broken refrigerator or microwave oven. Owing to her relative unfamiliarity with the neighborhood, she may have to run around several times before finding a skilled worker. If the worker is unable to fix the problem, she then has to contact the landlord and deal with him. "Living abroad alone really isn't easy," Belen says with a sigh. "We know so little about China… sometimes we're just like children. We face a lot of inconveniences and difficulties."

One time, Belen bought a round-trip air ticket for her boyfriend, who wanted to go back to Spain to visit his family. While she was tidying up the table at home just a few days before his flight, she mistook the ticket for garbage and ended up throwing it away. Belen and her boyfriend were extremely worried.

Belen had no choice but to call around asking how to replace the lost ticket. Since she and her boyfriend are foreigners, the procedures for replacing the air ticket were extremely complicated. They had to make a trip to the local police station to get a certificate, then go to the public security bureau to have the certificate stamped, and finally visit the airline company to obtain a replacement ticket. When they arrived at the company's office, they found out that the ticketing machine was broken and that they would have to wait several days before it was fixed. Though the timing was extremely tight, Belen managed to overcome multiple setbacks and get the ticket replaced in time for her boyfriend's flight home to Spain.

A tender love blossoms in China

While living abroad presents its share of inconveniences and difficulties for Belen, the companionship she receives from her boyfriend is a source of some solace and comfort.

Belen and her boyfriend grew up in the same city and have known each other since their high-school years, when they were innocent playmates. They went on to enroll in the same program at the same university. The only difference was their choice of a second language; Belen decided to study Chinese, while her boyfriend opted to study French. After graduation, Belen came to China to continue her studies. Her boyfriend, on the other hand, spent another year in Spain to learn French interpretation.

The beautiful and attractive Belen, however, would not be forgotten by her boyfriend. Just as soon as his studies were concluded, he got on a plane to visit his darling. The Spanish lovers then went on a journey to enjoy China's beautiful landscape and revel in their young love.

In order to remain with his beloved and, at the same time, fulfill his dream of living abroad, Belen's boyfriend decided to stay in Beijing. He received a job offer from a different department at Xinhua News Agency and became a colleague of Belen's at this prestigious news organization. Their

love was able to continue to grow and blossom in China.

Belen's boyfriend not only fully respects her wishes to study Chinese in depth, he is also mentally and spiritually supportive.

Not long ago, he changed his job and became a teacher at the Instituto Cervantes in Beijing, an organization established to enhance communication between Spain and China as well as to promote Spanish culture. This new job afforded him a flexible schedule which allowed him to do more translation work. It also gave him spare time to hire a Chinese teacher and begin learning Chinese.

"He has Chinese lessons twice a week," Belen says. "Every time he comes home, I become his 'private tutor.' He always asks me questions, like 'How do I write this word in Chinese?'—just like a little kid. Sometimes I intentionally test him with new words that he just learned, but he's usually too shy to answer. He's afraid that I'll laugh at him if he answers incorrectly."

I asked Belen whether it was her influence that her boyfriend started learning Chinese.

"He's been in China for three years and still can't speak Chinese... He's a bit embarrassed by this state of affairs," Belen replied half-jokingly. But she was also quick to praise her boyfriend. "His listening comprehension is really good. He's making rapid progress with the language."

In the exotic land of China, this congenial couple from Spain has not only created a romantic love story, but also gained an array of valuable knowledge and unforgettable experiences.

Far from home, Belen not only enjoys the companionship of her boyfriend, but also has the support and encouragement of her parents. Belen's father is a lawyer who runs his own law practice. Although Belen's parents miss her very much, they always have encouraging words for her, whether over the phone or during visits. "As long as this is what our daughter wants, we fully respect her decision," her parents say. "When we were young, we didn't have the chance to work abroad. For the younger generation, working in a foreign country and accumulating different life experiences will be of tremendous benefit."

By Liu Dongping
Translated by Matt

Personal File

Name: Igor Rogachev

Chinese Name: Luo Gaoshou

Nationality: Russian

Occupation: Diplomat

Time in China: 28 years

A Love of China that Never Fades

He is a kind and friendly old man, a man who has spent many years of his life in China, and who knows a great deal about this country. He even considers China his second homeland. He has witnessed the development of Sino-Soviet and Sino-Russian relations over many years, and promoted the friendship between the two nations. Now in his eighties, he still has a great dream—to further promote political, economic and cultural cooperation and development between the two countries. This man, an old friend of the Chinese people, is Igor Rogachev (or Luo Gaoshou in Chinese), the former Russian ambassador to China for more than 13 years.

"*I* have friends all over China. And I left with much sorrow. " Three years ago, a tall figure boarded a flight to Moscow. He was Igor Rogachev, who was leaving his post as Russian ambassador to China. But during these three years he appeared at Beijing Airport very often. This time he arrived as an overseas friend invited by the Chinese government to participate in the opening ceremony of the Beijing Olympics. "I'm very glad to be back in a place I am very familiar with," he said.

Igor Rogachev graduated in 1955 from the Moscow State Institute of International Relations of the USSR Ministry of Foreign Affairs. He was Russian Plenipotentiary to the People's Republic of China from 1992 to 2005. Just before the opening ceremony of the Olympic Games, we arranged a special interview with this "China expert" who worked in China three times for altogether 22 years.

Affection of a family of diplomats for China

After three years working in Moscow, the ex-diplomat came back to this land with which he has been connected for several decades. He appears with

the same bright smiles, the same fluent Chinese and the same expectations for friendship between China and Russia. But his spirits and responsibilities are different. Without the weight of the relationship between the two nations he used to shoulder in the past, he can enjoy the pleasure of life and the sweetness of friendship as much as he likes.

"As long as time permits, I will do my best to sense the changes in China. I can fully feel the profundity and greatness of this nation. It is a country that needs a lifetime of effort to understand." Igor Rogachev wrote in his autobiography. This affection toward China has not only lasted his entire diplomatic life but can also be traced back to the history of the Rogachev family as generations of diplomats.

Alexei Petrovich Rogachev, Igor's father, was a sinologist and diplomat who had a deep affection for China. His Chinese friends gave him a pure Chinese name, Luo Gaoshou, with a pronunciation similar to his Russian last name. When the son of Luo Gaoshou Sr. came to work in China, he inherited his father's Chinese name. Now few people in China really know his Russian name—Igor Alexeyvich Rogachev.

Igor's face turns solemn when recalling his father: "In 1924, when he came to China for the first time, he was an interpreter for the Soviet military adviser in Guangzhou. In 1927 the Guangzhou Uprising broke out. The Guangdong warlord captured several USSR personnel helping the Chinese Red Army. Fortunately my father and several other colleagues managed to escape in time. And that is why I am able to give this interview. The four captured USSR colleagues were killed. Now there are monuments to these four martyrs in the Guangzhou Uprising Martyrs Cemetery."

Even in a time filled with danger and turmoil, Igor's father chose to come to China, a land he was familiar with, once again with great resolution. "I lived in China soon after the moment I was born, so China is my first home country," said Igor. In 1932 Igor, still a three-month-old baby, came to Xinjiang with his parents. At the time, his father worked at the Consulate-general of the USSR in Dihua (now called Urumchi). "So when my Chinese friends ask me when I started learning Chinese. I will tell them jokingly that I started when I was three months old." So Igor's connection with China can be traced back to the time before the Second World War.

From 1936 to 1939 Igor's father was assigned to the USSR Consulate-general in Harbin, capital of Heilongjiang Province in Northeast China, then still under Japanese occupation. Speaking of his childhood during that period, Igor still remembers clearly: "One winter it was extremely cold. The temperature fell to minus 15 degrees. The Japanese military authorities blockaded the USSR Consulate-general, even stopping the water supply. All the Soviet personnel were forced to stay inside, and not allowed to go out to buy food and other things. At the time small children like me were told by our parents not to go out and walk in the snow, because they used to melt it for water. Fortunately our consul-general had good relations with the French consul-general. The latter would come by and bring some food for the children...." Igor looks completely calm when speaking of the hardship and turmoil in his childhood. We used to think the Russians were a nation of boldness, generosity, passion and masculinity. However, his calm and composed way of talking about difficulties shows grace and tolerance, and a heroic character. One always meets difficulties in life. Real bravery is to accept them without complaint or anger.

Later Igor's father returned to Moscow, but his affection for China did not

wane. "After his return to the USSR, my father taught Chinese language and literature at Moscow State University, and translated many Chinese classics into Russian. The most famous among them are *Journey to the West* and *The Outlaw of the Marsh*. Speaking of his father's literary attainments, the ambassador smiled a little. "The classics he translated sell well in Russia. Three reprints have been sold out since their first publication in the 1950s. Besides, he also translated many works of modern Chinese writers such as some of Lu Xun's short stories and Ding Ling's *The Sun over the Sanggan River*.

After Igor grew up, his father quickly passed his love for China, the Chinese people and Chinese culture and also his devotion to his diplomatic career to his son. Likewise, Igor has passed his affection for China to his own grandson.

Three generations of the ambassador's family—himself, his son and his grandson—all graduated from the Moscow State Institute of International Relations, the cradle of Russian diplomats. "My son is a diplomat. Now he is the deputy permanent representative of Russia to the United Nations. At the age of 45, he has deputy ambassador rank. So some times I tell him jokingly not to go higher than me."

He went on, "My grandson is 24 years old this year. He started to work for the Department of Justice, the Ministry of Foreign Affairs of Russia, after his graduation from the Moscow State Institute of International Relations. He specialized in International Law. When I worked as the Russian ambassador to China, I invited him to come and live

 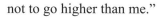

in Beijing for a few years. So he started speaking Chinese." Igor's eyes shine with happiness and pride, "In China you have a saying 'Like father, like son'. But for me I suggest it be changed to 'Like grandfather, like grandson'."

A witness to Sino-Russian relations

At the beginning of 1992, the first Russian president, Boris Yeltsin, signed a presidential order appointing Igor, the deputy minister of foreign affairs, ambassador extraordinary and plenipotentiary of the Russian Federation to China. From then on, Igor Rogachev became familiar to the Chinese people. But in fact he had already witnessed many historical moments in relations between China and the USSR since the early 1950s.

"In April 1956 I came to work in China, not long after the founding of the People's Republic of China," Igor said. In the five years he was here Igor Rogachev interpreted for Chinese leaders including Mao Zedong and Zhou Enlai. In the summer of 1956 he accompanied Soviet medical experts to investigate an epidemic of schistosomiasis in central China.

In January 1958 he was transferred to work at the Soviet Embassy in Beijing. He remembers that in November 1960 a reception was held at the embassy to celebrate the 43rd anniversary of the October Revolution. The guest of honor was Chairman Mao Zedong. Soviet Ambassador S.V. Chervonenko talked with Chairman Mao for one hour, and Igor translated for them. "The picture of us with Chairman Mao during this reception should be in the photo archives of Xinhua News Agency," he said.

In the summer of 1972, Igor Rogachev returned to Moscow. He was first a senior counselor in the Far Eastern Department of the Foreign Ministry,

Chairman Mao (fourth left), Zhou Enlai (second right) and Zhu De (first right) at the reception at the Soviet embassy in November 1960, Beijing.

and then was promoted to deputy director. Soon he was promoted to deputy minister of foreign affairs of the USSR. He worked under Minister Shevard-nadze (later president of Georgia) for five and a half years. He visited all the Asian countries, plus Australia and New Zealand, and accompanied President Gorbachev on his visits to Japan, South Korea, India and China. "The most important was the visit in May of 1989 to China, when Gorbachev met Deng Xiaoping," he noted. "At that time Deng Xiaoping lived in Shanghai, and the foreign minister and I went from Beijing to Shanghai to meet him, prior to Gorbachev's visit. The Chinese leader shook hands with the minister first and then with me, and said, 'I remember you. I have met you before. You were my interpreter during my talks with Soviet friends in the late 1950s.'

"After nearly a year of preparation work, Gorbachev finally met Deng Xiaoping in Beijing in May 1989. I was present during their meeting, and I shall always remember Deng Xiaoping's statement of great farsighted-ness: 'Let us end the past and open the future.' From then on the relationship between our two countries started to improve gradually. I believe that Deng was one of the most outstanding statesmen of the 20th century. The tremendous changes he brought to China's economy set a good example for the whole world. Many other countries are now learning from China's experience." Such cordial praise sounds like appreciation from one great man to another.

In the beginning of 1992 President Yeltsin signed a decree and sent the "China expert" to Beijing as Russian ambassador to China, a post he occupied for 13 years. During this period, what impressed him most was his personal participation in drafting the Sino-Russian Treaty of Good-Neighborly Relations, Friendship and Cooperation on July 16, 2001. "I discussed with my Chinese counterparts many times the basic concept of the treaty. We drafted each article carefully." As the ambassador to China he witnessed a milestone in Sino-Russian relations—the establishment of the Sino-Russian strategic cooperative partnership.

Igor Rogachev led the Russian delegation which negotiated the Supplementary Agreement on Eastern Section of the National Boundaries between Russia and China in October 2007. Recently, on July 21, 2008, Russia and China signed another important boundary demarcation protocol. It officially determines the 4,300-kilometer-long national boundaries between the two countries. Now the territorial issues between them are all settled." Luo still pays close attention to the development of the relationship between China and Russia, and continues to work for it. China is never been far away from his heart.

Many interesting stories of the ambassador

Igor Rogachev has had contacts and meetings with four generations of Chinese leaders, and he is proud to "have friends all over China". Together

with his humorous and flexible personality, his interesting interactions with his friends during his tenure added many funny stories to his 13 years of life as an ambassador.

"I often had dinner with Chinese friends. Once they came to my house and presented me with four bottles of wine. That wine was made of black ants and turtles and was very good for health. My friends said my hair would turn black if I drank it for long time. However, my hair has never turned black, although I have drunk it for several years."

Over the last three years he has visited China more than 20 times. He has been to the majority of the cities in China—from Heihe to Hainan and from Beijing to Hong Kong. And he knows the specialties of each of them. "Each autumn, ambassadors from various countries are attracted to the fashion festival held in Dalian," he noted. "The roast duck restaurants and the Laoshe Teahouse are places I often visit in Beijing, and I like swimming in the Ming Tombs Reservoir. I spend my vacation in Hainan during your Spring Festival each year. But now too many people go to Sanya. There is another beautiful place 20 kilometers from Sanya, and few people know it. It is a quiet place." He said that he once told the mayor of Sanya: "You Chinese say: 'Above is Paradise, and below are Suzhou and Hangzhou.' I want to change it to this: 'Above is Paradise, and below is Sanya'. "

Igor likes playing piano. He can play many Chinese songs on the piano such as *Unity Is Strength, I Am a Soldier.* When he worked at the embassy, Chinese radio and television stations often invited him to play Russian music. Bo Xilai, then mayor of Dalian, in Liaoning Province, proud of the fact that his province made the best pianos in China, once sent the ambassador a local piano as a present.

He recalled, "Two years ago I went to New York for an international conference. My son and his wife working there at the United Nations came to visit me. My son asked me to guide them around Chinatown, and there I was recognized by an old Chinese man, who greeted me as 'Ambassador Luo Gaoshou'. Surprised, I asked him how he knew me. He pointed at the television set in his shop, 'We watch news from China every day. You often appear on television, like a star.'"

From "official" ambassador to "folk" ambassador

I noticed that ex-ambassador Igor Rogachev has five mobile phones. Although he is no longer a diplomat he is still busy, having been elected in 2005 a senator of the upper house of the Russian parliament, the Federal

Meeting an old friend at the 15th China Harbin International Fair for Trade and Economic Cooperation.

Council of the Russian Federation. He represents the Amur region, which has the longest boundary line with China of all the Russian regions, at over 1,300 kilometers. The leaders and people of the Amur region are very interested in the cooperation with the neighboring provinces of China. During his ambassadorial career, Igor Rogachev met frequently with the leaders of China's northeastern provinces—Heilongjiang, Liaoning and Jilin—to promote cooperation and communication between the two sides. "The Amur region celebrated the 150th anniversary of its founding this year," Luo noted. "My biggest interest now is promoting the coordination of two great programs, Russia's Development of the Far East and Transbaikalia and China's Rejuvenation of old industrial bases in Northeast China."

Some time ago a delegation from the municipal government of Heihe, a city on the border between Heilongjiang and Siberia, visited Moscow and proposed that Heihe and its neighbor across the border, Blagoveschensk, establish a sister-cities relationship to build a "Heilongjiang Bridge", form an economic zone, and promote the further cooperation and development of their economies.

Igor has written a doctoral dissertation for the Moscow State Institute of International Relations. The title of his dissertation is *Sino-Russian Relations at the end of the 20th century and beginning of the 21st century.* "Three years ago, I published a book in Russian on this topic," he said, "containing articles I had written from 1972 to 2005. As a matter of fact, I could have got the degree of doctor of history in 1991, but just then President Yeltsin appointed me ambassador to China. Now I have a chance to get that degree after all."

After he returned to Moscow, Igor retained his Chinese lifestyle, and paid regular visits to Chinese restaurants in Moscow, of which there are about 100. Liu Guchang, the Chinese ambassador to Russia, introduced to him several Chinese restaurants. Igor Rogachev's house has Chinese things everywhere, including books, vases, works of calligraphy, paintings, Buddhist statues, carpets, teas and various kinds of Chinese liquor such as Maotai, Laobaigan and Shaoxing rice wine. His son collected about 100 Chairman Mao Zedong badges when he was in Beijing. "Many friends who have visited my house said it was like a museum after they saw so many Chinese things," he joked.

How to become an excellent diplomat

Not every diplomat can fit into his host country perfectly, like the way Igor Rogachev did. Igor said that he believes that the most important thing is to deeply understand the history, traditions, customs and national conditions of the host country, and the reforms and developments it has experienced. Then one can make an objective evaluation of the country, and analyze its internal and external policies objectively.

When this pleasant and successful interview ended, the words with which Ben Johnson once praised Shakespeare came into my mind: He is not of an age but for all time.

Maybe this can also be used to summarize the ambassador's career: He is not just an ambassador of our generation, but an example for generations of diplomats.

By Xu Yanzhuo and Xiao Lianbing
Translated by Xie Shengzhe

Personal File

Name: Carl Crook

Nationality: British

Occupation: Businessman

Time in China: 40 years

An Englishman Who Has Beijing at Heart

His parents were internationalists participating in the Chinese revolution. He was born in Beijing in 1949, and before the age of seven he could speak only Chinese. In the 1960s he went to high school in Beijing, and briefly became a Red Guard during the "cultural revolution". These fascinating experiences have captivated many people. After hearing him, everyone admires his authentic Beijing accent and regards him as a genuine Beijing native. In fact, he is a British man named Carl Crook. He works as the general manager of Montrose Food & Wine, a foreign company.

*C*arl Crook is a tall, a typical Westerner. Though a little introverted, once in conversation his fluent Beijing accent can surprise his listener. One of his friends said jokingly that when he speaks in Chinese people think someone else is doing the talking behind him. He speaks with a very native Beijing accent, and also he talks about "the foreigners" as if he were not one himself. When interviewed on TV lately, he was able to quote a few versus from Chairman Mao Zedong's poetry.

Now he lives in a renovated courtyard house near the western part of Beijing's Third Ring Road. As a matter of fact, Carl may have been one of the first foreigners to build a house in Beijing after the founding of New China in the year of his birth. He is very interested in Chinese culture and history, especially in the culture and history of Beijing. He is also fond of Chinese cuisine. He likes entertaining friends with roasted lamb and fine wines in his courtyard house. Talking about his own interest in food and wine, he said Donglaishun (a restaurant) on Wangfujing Street and the old Sichuan Fandian in Xirongxian Alley were two of his earliest memories of fine dining in old Beijing, and it might has been his father who influenced his taste for spicy Chinese foods.

Carl with his parents and two younger brothers in 1955.

China has been Carl's home on and off for almost 40 years. His father David Crook was born in London in 1910. He joined the International Brigade to fight in the Spanish civil war of 1936-1939, and was sent by the Communist International to China, where he met Isabel, daughter of a Canadian missionary and born in Chengdu. After their marriage, the couple went to the CPC's base area in the border regions of Shanxi, Hebei, Shandong and Henan. There they carried out research on land reform, and wrote a book *Revolution in a Chinese Village—Ten Mile Inn*. After the founding of New China, the couple helped the Chinese government to establish the Beijing Foreign Languages University. Now retired, Carl's mother is over 90 and she still lives on the campus of the university.

Carl did not follow in his parents' footsteps to be an educator, but became interested in the food and wine business. Carl recalled that in the 1950s, when he was four or five, his father sometimes took him by pedicab to Donglaishun on Wangfujing Street. At that time Donglaishun served customers very big hot pots with partition screens around them, and a group of strangers ate at the same table out of their respective compartments from the same hot pot. This rather un-extravagant eating style was Carl's first memory of one of his favorite Beijing dishes.

Carl first attended Chongwen Primary School, and later enrolled at the Affiliated High School of Peking University. There was a period of food shortage in the 1960s, and some of the foreigners in China got to experience the taste of "recall bitterness meals", which were intended to recall the "bitter" past. "Recall bitterness meals" were made of coarse grains like sorghum, corn meal and husks, which was pretty rough fare. "No too appetizing", said Carl.

Red Guard Carl Crook was worried despite his well-off life

Soon after the "cultural revolution" started in 1967, Carl's parents were arrested on spying charges. Despite the sadness of being separated from his parents, Carl still managed to enjoy freedom from paternal supervision. He and his brothers continued to receive his parents' salaries every month, totalling 360 yuan, which at that time was a very substantial amount compared with an ordinary worker's salary of 30 yuan to 40 yuan. During this period Carl found the time and funds to explore the interesting sites around the city of Beijing and also to dine with friends at the famous restaurants in the city, which were not that many nor expensive in those days. No wonder his recollections of that period are still fond ones.

Carl joined in the Red Flag Group organized by the Red Guards in the Affiliated High School of Peking University, but being a foreigner, he was primarily an observer. "As foreigners, we were rather marginalized at the time. I only took part in meetings, no violent incidents." Carl said that his home and some of their family possessions were subject to search and seizure by other Red Guards.

Carl in Anyuan, Jiangxi Province, during the "cultural revolution".

In 1969, his classmates all went to rural areas, and he and his brother were first assigned to work at the Haidian Agricultural Machinery Repair and Fittings Factory for two years, and then to the Beijing No.1 Auto Repair Factory for another two years. Carl recalled that those days were not that bad in his memory. His fellow workers were friendly, and people do tend to enjoy memories of their youth. He remembered clearly that when US President Nixon visited China, he and his co-workers were awakened at four in the morning to clear snow from the road to the Badaling Great Wall, which Nixon was to visit.

Thanks to Premier Zhou Enlai's personal intervention, his parents were freed in 1973. Carl recollected that at a reception specially held at Great Hall of the People, Premier Zhou apologized to all those foreign experts who had been arrested, toasted their families and said that he hoped the incident would not leave them with a bad memory of China. Carl said his parents never had any regrets about coming to China, even after spending years in prison.

Though he did not suffer much in the "cultural revolution", his feelings about it are not all that easy. He explained, "Although I did not suffer any material deprivation during the 'cultural revolution', as the years wore on I was somewhat depressed." Looking back on the situation, he said he did not simply see the "cultural revolution" as a spontaneous mass movement reflecting the struggle between different political lines; it was orchestrated from

Carl with his brothers and friends in the Western Hills, Beijing.

the top down for the purpose of political struggle. Once the movement got started, it quickly got out of control as many people tried to use the turmoil to address personal grievances and ambitions.

Carl said, "Mentioning the 'cultural revolution', everyone claims to be a victim, but many people should also take the responsibility for the roles they played as persecutors. Years later, I ran into members of the Red Guards who searched my home during the 'cultural revolution', but I have yet to hear an apology from them," he noted. Talking about how the Chinese people can properly assess the effects of the "cultural revolution", he said that the

Carl with friends who saw him off at Beijing Railway Station when he left China in 1973.

American Civil War caused over one million deaths out of a total population of 25 million, far more traumatic than the "cultural revolution", and Americans took generations to come to terms with the scars left by that conflict. So maybe China will go though a similar process in understanding the "cultural revolution".

Learning English while visiting relatives overseas

Three months after his parents were freed in 1973, Carl left China. But he was never to be disconnected from China for long. In 1974, with the help of his friend Marni, who became his wife, the two went to study at the University of Massachusetts, where he got a master's degree in education. After this, Carl was accepted by Stanford University and got a master's degree in East Asian Studies. He never finished his Ph.D. in Chinese history, so he is reluctant to call himself a China scholar.

Carl hardly learnt any English before the age of seven. He explained that his parents were both English teachers at the Beijing Foreign Languages University, so they didn't speak Chinese very well, but to make sure that their children would speak Chinese fluently, they only spoke Chinese at home. As a

A boss who loves wine culture.

result, when Carl went with his family to Canada and Britain to visit relatives in 1957, he had to study English from scratch. When he arrived in Vancouver as a child, he spoke Chinese to his brothers in a taxi. The taxi driver, who happened to be Chinese, was greatly startled to hear foreign-looking children speak fluent Chinese. Carl did not really immerse himself in an English-language atmosphere until he went to college in the US.

Apart from language, Carl is also steeped in Chinese culture. He said, "Even as a child I was constantly reminded of the fact that I was a foreigner, but I still feel a very strong identity with Chinese culture. Chinese can be called my mother tongue and Beijing is my native place." But Carl also has a great fondness for his other home in America, which has very beautiful natural surroundings, and he often wishes he could spend more time there. He feels fortunate that his parents raised him equally in the two great cultural heritages, Chinese and English.

Reform and opening-up brought him the chance to get into the wine business

When Carl returned to China in 1984 he became the director of the Beijing liaison office of the Occidental Petroleum Corporation, in charge of coal mining business. With his familiarity with China, he was quickly able to build working relations, and greatly enjoyed the work. Four years later, there was a huge drop in coal prices on the international market, and the US partner withdrew from the joint venture. Carl went back to America, to do consultancy business related to China. Then he came back to Beijing, and worked here for a British company dealing with transnational transportation

for more than two years.

After working in the coal business in China for five years, Carl spend a few years back in the US, then in 1994 he started a joint-venture packaging company in China with an American friend, but due to many difficulties the packaging business was not successful. However, his American partner was very fond of fine wine, and since China had very little imported wine at that time they decided to import and distribute wines in China. Their wine business grew rapidly. That was the beginning of Carl's career in the wine business. From then on, Carl developed a great interest in wines. He said, "We were one of the first foreign companies to import and distribute wines in China. Things were very different then; there were not many wine companies. Now there are dozens of importers distributing thousands of different imported wines in the Chinese market. The competition is fierce." Carl also helped popularize knowledge of viniculture. He helped to translate and publish many articles on the subject in China. Gradually, wine is being accepted by more and more restaurants in Beijing.

To many of his friends, Carl's interest in wine is not just about business. "Wine should not become an object for conspicuous consumption in China. Nor should wine drinking take the 'bottoms up' tradition of Chinese spirits," he said. "Wine should be consumed in moderation. It should be savored and matched with food for full enjoyment. The story of wine is so rich that the more one learns about wine, the more fascinating it is. It would be a great shame to have it consigned to the role of extravagant display."

Carl said the current per capita consumption of wine in China is only one tenth of the world's average, so the Chinese market still has great potential. "One thing is sure, ten years from now the Chinese will drink more wine than now. Now that Beijing is fast becoming one of the great international cosmopolitan centers of the world, the availability of a rich selection of wines from around the world is becoming all the more important."

Looking back on his recent years in China, he expresses some regrets about lacking the spirit of dedication of his parents. He often asks himself what he has done for China, because he is a beneficiary of the reform and opening-up policies. He spoke of his interest in the preservation of Beijing's historical buildings and traditional culture. He used to write to the city government to express his concern for the preservation of the old courtyards. In other respects, he believes his wine business, which employs close to a hundred people, has not only helped to enrich the quality of life in Beijing, it also provides job opportunities.

Stumbling on a bodega

More than ten years ago Carl bought a dilapidated courtyard near Purple Bamboo Park in the western part of Beijing. Then he renovated the old courtyard in the traditional Chinese architectural style. He still has the faded old deeds of the house carrying the seal of the then mayor. His new deeds have the serial number: Waizhunzi 001, indicating that it is the first property in this category. He said with pride that he is probably the first foreigner to build a house in

Relaxing in his own bodega.

Beijing in recent years.

As a matter of fact, it was not easy for him to get the No.001 house. In March 1989, Carl, who was close to 40, wanted to buy a courtyard house. He had always wanted to have his own house in Beijing, but his various applications to buy a house were unsuccessful because foreigners had not been given the right to purchase property at the time. Then he came up with the idea of buying a house in the name of his mother.

Though without Chinese nationality, Carl's mother has made great contributions to China, and has been awarded the title of Honorary Citizen of Beijing. With this title, he bought the house in his mother's name, and in later years the title was transferred to himself.

In 1999, during a conversation with an old neighbor, he found out that there were cellars under the house, though he was not clear as to its actual location. After some weeks of exploration, Carl finally found the entrance to this mysterious catacomb of small cellars.

He connected the cellar to his basement with a flight of wooden stairs. Descending into the cellar, you will see several small rooms. In the middle room, Carl has built some brick shelves, where he has stored dozens of bottles of wine. The other rooms are mostly empty, except for one where he put a number of stone Buddhist statues; in the last room, there is a wooden table with carved patterns which carried thread-bound classic books and the four treasures of the study (writing brush, ink stick, ink slab, and paper), and a hollow iron lamp hanging overhead with a little door through which a candle can be put in the lamp. The temperature in the cellar stays at around 16℃, which is perfect for wine storage.

He was very pleased with this discovery. Though he is not a religious man, he thought this was a gift from Heaven. He said after years in the wine business, he had always wanted to have a wine cellar. He only had to do very little work to fix up the cellar. "If I had to build such a cellar from scratch, it would have cost me a fortune," he noted.

The pleasures of Chinese courtyard living

High residential towers have been built near Carl's courtyard in recent years. Just to the north is the Changhe Canal, a waterway flowing from the Summer Place to the heart of the old city. At his front gate is a plane tree, its leaves rustling in the wind. Though not far from the Third Ring Road, the courtyard is a very peaceful place where you can see Chinese dates hanging high in the date trees and wisteria clinging around. The windows and doors of

A quiet courtyard away from downtown.

the house are built with wooden lattice in the traditional Chinese style, antique and elegant. All these things would not suggest that this is the home of a foreign family. In the courtyard there is an oven built in the form of a well. The thermometer beside it can monitor the temperature in the oven. In the cooler months, Carl will sometimes roast whole lambs in this oven, and entertain his friends with wine. Many visitors have been Carl's friends since he was

Carl's parents in the Shanxi-Hebei-Shandong-Henan Border Area.

young, and many of them are also descendants of revolutionaries. Carl told me that sometimes a group of them will sing model opera tunes from the "cultural revolution" period together. "It does strike people as odd to see a group of foreigners singing Chinese Opera," he mused.

The living room of the house rises to the ceiling through both storeys of the building, with sunlight pouring in from widows on both floors, making the room very bright. On the right of the living room sits a wooden carving of the pot-bellied Maitreya, giving a jovial air to the room, and making it seem unlikely to belong to a foreigner. Most noticeable in the living room are black-and-white pictures of Carl's parents. One of these shows Carl's parents when they were young in the Shanxi-Hebei-Shandong-Henan Border Area. They are both wearing the thick clothes typical of Chinese revolutionary families at that time.

Carl said that times have changed greatly since his parents came to

Beijing, but they remained faithful to their socialist ideas. They were happy to see the growing prosperity, but still concerned with the progress of social justice and equality. Carl believes that the economic prosperity of recent years is already a great achievement.

Regret that his sons did not go through some years of Chinese school

On the bookshelf of the second floor there are lots of Chinese books and many of them are thread-bound ones in traditional Chinese characters. Among them, books on Chinese history account for a large part. These books are not just for decoration, as Carl is familiar with a great number of the books, for example, he was able to cite many interesting facts from the book *Construction Rules and Examples of the Qing Dynasty* by Liang Sicheng, such as the names of various parts of ancient buildings, and it is this very book that helped him renovate his courtyard house. "The rafter is made of fir, the purline yellow pine, the crossbeam pine, the window lattice from Qiumu, and the floor from oak," said Carl in an enthusiastic tone.

Carl's knowledge of Chinese history and culture surprises many Chinese people. He recounted one of his adventures, when he accidentally discovered the ancient battlefield of Tumubao.

Carl's mother is in her nineties and still lives a healthy and active life in her apartment at the Beijing Foreign Languages University. Carl visits his mother every week. Carl's three sons all study abroad. Every year they gather in Beijing during their school holidays.

"I enjoy my Chinese cultural heritage, and sometimes I wish I had passed on more of it to my sons. Chinese is a second language to them, so

Carl with his mother (front right), his wife (front left), sons (second right and left rear), and two brothers (first and third left rear).

maybe I should have raised them in the way my parents raised me," Carl said.

His sons are studying either engineering or environmental sciences, and so far none of them seems interested in wine.

Mentioning the 2008 Beijing Olympics, Carl said regretfully that he had missed it because he was abroad at the time. However, he said he did meet an English journalist who had covered ten Olympic games since 1972 and shared the same feelings about Beijing Olympics as Carl. The journalist said in Beijing he experienced the most wonderful Olympics, not because it had a magnificent opening ceremony, but because Chinese people were so hospitable and the volunteers were so excellent. Carl thought the Beijing Olympics was very successful. As a British man, he believed the 2012 Olympics would be quite different, and given a chance he would love to be in London for the event.

By Shan Jinliang
Translated by Zhang Ruiqing

Personal File

Name: Antonio Fernandez Arce

Nationality: Peruvian

Occupation: Journalist

Time in China: 30 years

A Half-Century Attachment to China

Antonio Fernandez Arce, a 77-year-old Peruvian, has had a legendary experience working in China as an expert. Over 40 years ago, when he first visited China, he had the great honor to shake hands with Chairman Mao Zedong. During the turbulent "cultural revolution", Premier Zhou Enlai personally dictated arrangements that saved his little daughter's life. In the early 1970s, he was entrusted as a secret messenger between China and Peru for setting up formal diplomatic ties.

He has cherished a profound attachment to China for half a century, and nourished deep "blood is thicker than water" feelings for the country.

Your ancient Inca Empire was marvelous, Chairman Mao told him

Flashback to the early 1950s.

It was in Lima, the capital of Peru, a South American country far away from China. Young journalist Antonio Fernandez Arce was an active, charismatic figure in the press. His outstanding journalistic feats brought him to the chair of the National Association of Journalists of Peru at the age of 25. At the same time, he was charged with the preparations for the establishment of the Latin American Journalists Association.

Arce wanted very much to know what was going on in the newborn China. He and some progressive young Peruvians formed a Peru-China friendship association. They tried in many ways to amass all possible information on New China in hopes of setting up friendly ties with it through non-governmental channels. As the chairman of Peru's Journalists Association, he had the privilege of attending some international journalism conventions. It was during one of these conferences that he had an unexpected chance to get his first contact with new China.

In October 1960 he attended a world conference of journalists held in

Vienna, the capital of Austria. It was his first time to meet journalists from the People's Republic of China. He still remembers that among those present at the conference were Deng Tuo, chairman of the All-China Journalists Association, and Jin Zhonghua, founder and director of the magazine *China Today*. He had a cordial conversation with his Chinese colleagues.

During the conference he received invitations to visit many countries, including the Soviet Union, Hungary, Czechoslovakia and China. "But my first choice was China. Since then, many Chinese colleagues of the older generation have become good friends of mine," he recalled with pleasure.

In the winter of the same year, he came to China with a dozen colleagues from Brazil, Peru, Bolivia and other Latin American countries.

He was lucky enough on his very first visit to the country to be received

In 1960 Arce was received by Chairman Mao Zedong.

by Chairman Mao Zedong and other state leaders.

That unforgettable event still remains fresh in his mind.

"Our car drove into Zhongnanhai. In a spacious meeting hall we saw the chairman, whom we had been aspiring to see for a long time. Premier Zhou and Foreign Minister Chen Yi were also present. Chairman Mao was the founder of New China, and he enjoyed great prestige among us progressive Latin American youths, too."

To his surprise, the chairman was not only interested in the situation in Latin America, but also very familiar with its history. Arce still remembers that, soon after the meeting started, Chairman Mao said, "The exchanges and understanding between our two sides are far from being enough since Latin America is far from China. And you are our best teachers to help us understand Latin America better. That is why we invited you to visit."

Then the Chairman turned to Arce, who was sitting beside him, and said, "You are from Peru. The Inca Empire in ancient Peru was marvelous. It had advanced agriculture, superior architectural arts and rich astronomical knowledge. It was also said to be a society with strict moral standards."

"No stealing, no lying and no sluggishness" were the three moral standards the Inca people of all generations embraced, Arce answered. The chairman repeated the three standards, and nodded. "What high moral standards they are!" he said.

Arce and all the others present were moved by the Chairman's cordial words. And they all admired the chairman's rich historical knowledge of Peru.

We can imagine how excited Arce was with his first visit to the faraway mysterious country.

Arce visited China in the 1960s.

Regardless of the biting cold in the early morning, he climbed to the roof of the Beijing Hotel, and looked around. Within his panoramic view were the Tiananmen Gate Tower shining golden in the morning sun; the ancient city walls far into the distance; the awe-inspiring Forbidden City; the magnificent Zhengyangmen Gate; and the dignified Temple of Heaven, all reflecting the splendid history of the ancient city.

Walking down Chang'an Avenue, a busy thoroughfare of the city, Arce experienced the orchestra of cars honking and crowds of bicycles. Outside the Qianmen Gate, he even saw a camel caravan. In factories and fields he felt the great enthusiasm of workers and farmers to build the country as masters of the new society. In schools and children's palaces, he found the lively youngsters were vibrant and full of vigor.

These vivid scenes converged in his mind and formed an image of an old country revitalized with youth and vigor.

Since then Arce has been bonded to the ancient country in the Far East. He would come to China for a visit whenever it was possible. When he was on vacation, he would come to cover news events in China and conduct interviews with Chinese people. Based on his own experience, he wrote numerous reports on China for Latin American news media. Before long, he was publicly recognized as the most prolific reporter specializing in Chinese affairs.

Running in his daughter's veins are the Premier's tender care and soldiers' blood

In March 1966, Arce visited China again, at the invitation of the All-China Journalists Association. Atop the Tiananmen Gate Tower, he met Chairman Mao for the second time. Then he traveled widely in China, and collected information for his news reports. When the other delegates left for home he decided to stay behind. Since he had brought with him large quantities of works of Peruvian folk art, he hoped to show Peruvian artistic culture to the Chinese people. In his spare time after news reporting, he contacted the related departments for the preparation of a Peruvian folk art exhibition. At his own expense, the exhibition was held in the Working People's Cultural Palace in Beijing. Chu Tunan, chairman of the Chinese People's Association for Friendship with Foreign Countries, attended the opening ceremony, and China's Central News Film Studio shot a special documentary of the exhibition. He keeps a copy of the ten-minute newsreel.

In 1967, he came to China once again by himself. This time he worked as an expert in the Spanish Department of Radio Beijing, which is now China

Radio International. At that time the country was in great disorder, as it was undergoing the "cultural revolution". Many foreigners packed up and left for home. Arce was probably the only Peruvian to stay behind. He stayed because he wanted to know more about the country and collect more information for his future books on China.

His first wife came to join him in Beijing. Their daughter Mei Mei was born in Beijing in 1970. Not long after she was born, the baby suffered septicemia and was rushed to the Beijing Children's Hospital in a critical condition. At that time, Arce was busy translating documents for an important conference of the Communist Party of China. The translators worked behind closed doors in a suburb of Beijing, and were not allowed to go home.

Just at this time, Premier Zhou came to visit the foreign experts. During their conversation, the interpreter told the premier that the Peruvian expert's daughter, who had contracted a serious disease, was in hospital for emergency treatment. Thereupon, the premier ordered the top military doctors to take special measures to treat the baby.

Mei Mei needed a blood transfusion, but there was not enough matching plasma in the hospital's blood bank. The medical department in charge immediately contacted the army for help. Many soldiers, upon hearing the news, rushed to the hospital to donate blood, and the little girl eventually pulled through after having had a close brush with death.

Occupied with myriads of state affairs as he was, Premier Zhou ordered his aides to inquire frequently about the baby's condition. Only when the girl had completely recovered and been discharged from the hospital, did the premier set his mind at ease. He also asked someone to congratulate Arc on Mei Mei's return to health.

Arce with Zhou Enlai in 1960.

Arce is stirred emotionally whenever he recalls the touching anecdote. He told us that Premier Zhou showed great solidarity with the people regarding their hardships and sufferings. His lofty moral character was on everybody's lips.

Arce said, "Who would think that he could care for a foreign child with as much thoughtful attention as his own flesh and blood? The great Premier of China gave Mei Mei a new life. My family will never forget that."

He had another unforgettable episode when he met the Premier for the first time.

It happened during his first visit to China. When he arrived at the place where Chairman Mao was to receive him, Arce was greeted by a very polite official before they went into the meeting hall. The gentleman came to the car to shake hands with Arce and the others with him. When he asked his interpreter to introduce the premier to him, he was told that the official who had

shaken hands with him was none other than the premier himself.

Upon hearing this, Arce wasted no time to give the Premier his best regards and apologize. He told the Premier that when they shook hands, he took him for a protocol officer and did not show the due honor to him. He begged pardon for his negligence and disrespect.

"Never mind," the Premier said, laughing heartily. "Now we know each other. We both have the feeling of 'regret for not having met earlier'. That shows we are true friends." The Premier's profound words, generosity and refined manners drew Arce's admiration.

When they got the sad and startling news of the premier's death on January 8, 1976, the Arce family, now back in Peru, was deeply grieved. Arce and Mei Mei hurried to the Chinese Embassy in Lima to express their deep condolences. They stood in front of the Premier's portrait in silent tribute to the great man. They left a message in the condolence book expressing their memories of the deceased, who had been the savior of Arce's daughter.

Time elapsed, and Mei Mei grew up and became a mother herself. The grown-up Mei Mei has a deeper understanding of her special ties with the premier. On the 50th anniversary of the People's Republic of China, she wrote an article specially for the occasion. The article, titled, "China in my blood and in my heart," conveyed her boundless gratitude to the country and to the late premier.

A secret messenger for Sino-Peruvian diplomatic relations

At the end of 1970 Arce received a letter telling him that his father was seriously ill and hoped he would go back to see him. Arce asked Radio

Beijing for leave.

Before his departure, he was invited by Jiao Ruoyu, who later became the first Chinese ambassador to Peru, to have tea together with Premier Zhou. During their conversation, the premier expressed China's wish to increase its contacts with Peru. He put forth "Eight Principles" for the establishment of diplomatic relations between the two countries. Among the eight principles were the famous Five Principles of Peaceful Coexistence. The Premier hoped that Arce, who was the only Peruvian working and living in China, would deliver in person the eight principles to the Peruvian government authorities.

Entrusted by the Chinese premier, Arce set out on the journey via Hong Kong, together with his wife and two daughters. They had some trouble on their entry into Hong Kong, as Mei Mei, who was only eight months old, didn't have a Peruvian passport. With only a copy of her China-issued birth certificate she was not allowed to enter the British colony. After a few days, a guarantee by the Peruvian consul-general in Hong Kong secured their entry.

Soon after he arrived in Hong Kong, Arce had a long conversation with the Peruvian consul-general throughout the night. The consul-general reported this matter to his government, and so when Arce's plane landed in Lima a special car dispatched by the president's office was waiting for him at the airport.

The car took the family immediately to the president's office. The vice-president met and talked with Arce after receiving from him a memorandum containing China's Eight Principles. He also relayed Premier Zhou's sincerity and viewpoints.

Then he returned to his hometown to see his father. On the seventh day after his arrival the president's office summoned him to Lima for a detailed

discussion. Government officials told him that the Peruvian government agreed fully with the Eight Principles, and planned to have further discussions with the Chinese side. However, they swore him to secrecy over the matter.

In April 1971, a five-member official delegation from China headed by Deputy Minister of Foreign Trade Zhou Huamin visited Peru. At the welcoming ceremony at the airport, a Peruvian government official formally declared that Peru agreed fully with China's Eight Principles for establishing Sino-Peruvian diplomatic relations. The Peruvian side gave a copy of the declaration to the Chinese delegation. Shortly afterwards, the news was published around the world.

Arce accompanied the Chinese delegation as a tour guide to many places of interest. The name Peru, Arce told the Chinese, was derived from Quechua, a local native language, and meant "big ear of corn". He also introduced to the delegation the splendor of the Inca Empire in the period from the 12th to the 16th centuries, and the ancient capital Cuzco, which was known by the Incas as the "center of the universe".

During the visit, the two sides reached an agreement to set up a commercial representative office in each other's capital.

Two months later, Arce was dispatched to Beijing once again as an adviser to the Peruvian Commercial Representative Office in China. He worked hard to promote foreign trade and the establishment of formal ties with China. Peru received steady business orders from China. In the first year alone, the country exported 150,000 tons of fish meal, 20,000 tons of fish oil, 40,000 tons of copper, 10,000 tons of lead and 10,000 tons of zinc to China.

In Arce's words, the office was actually Peru's "embassy ad interim".

Its staff members were not only in charge of economic affairs but also of the intense preparations for establishing diplomatic relations with China. Just six months after the representative office was set up, the two countries formalized their diplomatic relations, on November 2, 1971.

That day, a grand banquet was held to celebrate the event in a large, splendidly decorated restaurant. Chinese Foreign Minister Qiao Guanhua attended. Arce was also present as a distinguished guest. The guests raised their glasses, and proposed toasts to the friendship between the two peoples.

Before long, the representative office in each other's country was changed to an embassy. And in the same year, China's legitimate seat at the United Nations was restored, resulting in many nonaligned countries recognizing China and establishing diplomatic relations with it.

"I think you have become an international fighter for criticism"

Arce returned home in 1973, and was appointed director of the editorial department of *News Daily*. He still kept his eyes on developments in China. He used to cover and comment on any major event that happened in the country. The Western media liked to picture China with biased reports and viewpoints. As a witness to the social progress in China, Arce would refute these reports with facts he had experienced or seen with his own eyes. The numerous articles, commentaries and reports he wrote on China were convincing and well received by his readers. They were not only carried by Peru's newspapers and magazines, but also published in other South American countries as well as in Spain. In those years, Arce was a noted "Columnist on China" within the Latin American media.

In 1979 Li Xiannian and other Chinese leaders received Arce.

On October 6, 1976, the Gang of Four was smashed, and removed from their positions. China was about to usher in a new historical epoch. Arce, still far away in Peru, followed this great event with acute perception. In April 1977 he came to China for a visit along with the chairman of the Peru-China Friendship Association.

As an old friend who had worked and lived in the country, Arce believed he had the responsibility to report the truth about China. To tell the truth was a counter-attack against the anti-China forces of the Western media. It was helpful to clarify misunderstandings about China among the Peruvian people and the people of the other Latin American countries. He hoped to acquaint himself with a thorough, in-depth knowledge of the country, and to write first-hand impartial reports on China to ensure correct understanding.

He met Chinese Vice-premier Li Xiannian. Li, an easy-going leader, had a humorous style of conversation, and helped him clear up any doubts and misgivings in his mind.

Arce told the vice-premier that he was disgusted with the excesses in criticizing Marshal Chen Yi at the beginning of the "cultural revolution". He couldn't understand why Jiang Qing, Mao's wife, controlled the literary circles with only eight so-called model dramas and why they did not allow Radio Beijing to broadcast beautiful Latin music. "Now I understand what they did is called 'going against the tread of the times'," he said. Hearing this, the vice-premier, bursting into laughter, said, "I think you have become an international fighter for criticism."

Arce had a long-cherished dream: to write a book on China based on what he had heard and seen. It was impossible to realize his dream during the "cultural revolution". Now that the revolution was over, it had become possible.

He had a very tight schedule visiting and meeting during the day, and sorting out his notes during the evening. He grasped every possible minute during his visit to write a large number of reports on China after Mao Zedong.

He compiled these reports and articles into a book, titled "Post-Mao China". It was a valuable tool for Spanish-speaking readers to better understand China, and therefore was well received in Latin American countries.

He heartily rejoices at every item of good news about China

In 1983 he found himself on his way to China again. This time, he was

engaged as a Spanish-language expert in the International News Department of Xinhua News Agency, where he worked for more than ten years. To his delight, at the agency he learned a lot from reading Xinhua news dispatches every day.

It was imperative for China to adopt its reform and open-door policies, as Arce saw it. He said, "It was the true starting point for China to achieve its magnificent goal of the Four Modernizations, though Premier Zhou had brought up this plan a long time before, in the sixties. Mao Zedong concluded that in China, where feudalism had ruled for such a long time, the people and the whole society should adapt their minds, their viewpoints and their ideology to the new times."

Living and working in the country that had undergone a reform and

Arce with his wife.

opening-up transition, he did not follow the steps of foreign media and confine his attention to surface phenomena. He attached a great importance to the root causes and the in-depth historical and cultural backgrounds of the social and political changes. Working at the news agency, he believed, was helpful for him to get to know the country much better.

It was during this period that he got his new romance. In 1985, at a dance party, he met a Beijing lady who had just returned from studying abroad. They were attracted to each other, and fell in love instantly. They ended up in a happy marriage. His wife became his right-hand help in work and care, tender in his day-to-day life. Family happiness has brightened his life in China.

The great changes that took place with each passing day left a deep impression on him. While doing his routine work, Arce made the best use of his time conducting interviews and collecting related information. Based on these interviews and information, he wrote a large amount of objective reports on China, and published them in Latin America and Spain.

Even while he was in hospital for a time, he still worked at his type-writer. When he finished an article he would call his wife to the hospital to collect it and send it out, no matter how late it was. One day, he sent his wife to the telegraph office to have an article transmitted, even though it was pouring with rain outside. She understood very well that news was of the utmost importance to her husband, who was dedicated to his news career.

In their home, she showed us many of her husband's works. Among them were articles on the Three-Gorges Dam, Shenzhou Spacecraft, and so on. The one that caught our attention was an album of pictures, titled "The Outlook for China in the New Era". It had been published by a Colombian

company in Chinese, English and Spanish. In the words of a Mexican critic, the album, with beautiful pictures and excellent accompanying text, was "an all-around introduction to China". With detailed and accurate descriptions of Chinese culture, history and customs, it was "the best gateway to knowledge the country for foreigners".

In 2004, after a couple of years in Peru, he came back to Beijing and was engaged as a senior advisor to the CCTV Spanish-language channel. He worked hard as usual for China's journalism and cultural exchanges with foreign countries. China's State Administration of Foreign Experts Affairs cited him as a "Foreign Expert with Outstanding Contributions" for his notable accomplishments.

His love of China comes from his heart. He would be heartily jubilant whenever there was good news. When China won the bid for the 2008 Olympic Games, entered the WTO or launched the Shenzhou Spacecraft, for example, the excited Arce worked late into the night to send the good news to his Latin American readers. Even when he was aboard a plane, he would collect any news he heard for his future reports.

Two years ago, when he was again in Peru, the country's leading TV network interviewed him. The first question was, "As a Peruvian who has lived and worked in China for years, would you please tell us why the country has achieved such rapid economic and social development in recent years?"

"It is simply a miracle that China has achieved its great accomplishments in only a quarter of a century," he answered. "These miraculous achievements are unique in the world."

One important reason was that the country had a very solid political foundation, i.e., the stability and solidarity of its people. This was the fundamental guarantee for implementing its reform and opening-up policies, he continued.

His legendary experience in China is strong evidence of the long-lasting friendship between China and Peru.

Now Arce has settled down in his new home in Beijing's Shijicheng neighborhood. Beijing has become his second home. He still reads and writes about China, which he finds is an endless topic for him.

By Liu Dongping
Translated by Yang Yaohua

Personal File

Name: Ulrich Kausch

Chinese Name: Kang Lichen

Nationality: German

Occupation: Director of Shenzhen Jade
Cargo Airlines CEO office

Time in China: 13 years

My Happy Life in China

It was in this country that Ulrich Kausch mastered the Chinese language, met his better half, and formed a family. It was here that he learned to be an upright person….

He is a young German who had romantic notions about the big country in the East and its ancient culture when he was a kid. Many of his dreams have come true. But he has yet to achieve the biggest one—to express his thoughts in Chinese.

"My Chinese name is Kang Li Chen. Kang means health in Chinese, Li means standing and Chen means morning," he explained in fluent Chinese with charming wit when we exchanged greetings.

Ulrich Kausch, director of Shenzhen Jade Cargo Airlines CEO office, introduced himself with a sunny smile.

Chinese has rendered my life colorful

Ulrich has been attached to China for more than ten years, though he is only in his early thirties.

He got his first chance to visit China after graduation from college in 1995.

"At that time, I traveled a lot on business with my boss. One day, my boss told me that I should have a Chinese name. Then I pointed randomly at a name in a Chinese telephone book and told him I would take that one. 'That doesn't suit you,' he said. 'You choose one for me then,' I suggested. 'All right,' he replied. He went back to his office and came out about an hour later. 'Kang Lichen. That's your Chinese name,' he said."

"I asked him the meaning of it. 'You have been here in China for several

months and have never been sick,' he explained. 'You seem very healthy, so your last name is Kang, which means health in Chinese. Your first name is Lichen; Li means standing. When we have discussions, you always stand your ground for what you think is right, not too radical and not giving way too easily. In Chinese, you are said to stand in the right place. Chen means early morning. You are always the first to come to the office and work hard.' I thought the name was not so bad, so I adopted it with delight."

With the Chinese name Kang Lichen, he has happily and cheerfully conducted his business in many parts of this country.

Later, he worked for awhile in Shenzhen and Zhuhai as a project manager for an IT company. It was during this period that he gradually realized that it was far from being enough to have a Chinese name only. Instead, it was most important to have a deep understanding of the country and its culture.

"I was too young and thought pretty highly of myself. With the experience working in a Mississippi IT company, I found the work at the Shenzhen IT business not very challenging. I drew up a plan to be carried out in a top-down approach. The plan ended in failure. I blamed the Chinese employees for it, thinking they were clumsy and too slow in understanding. I asked my boss to fire them, and got a new group for the plan. But it turned out to be a failure again. Only by this time did I realize that there was probably something wrong with me."

He came to the awareness that he only had two choices: To leave China for good and seek a job somewhere else, or stay in China and accommodate himself to the country with a quicker and better understanding of it.

He chose the latter without the least hesitation. He immediately engaged

a teacher to teach him Chinese in his office after work. "The Chinese employees changed their attitude when they saw the teacher walking into my office. The next morning, when I greeted them with 'hello' in Chinese, they seemed delighted. They looked at me in a different way when they understood that I really wanted to get a better knowledge of their country with concrete actions."

Ulrich has since been studying Chinese untiringly. "I would have only the two colors of black and white in my work and life in China if I only spoke English. But my life here has been more colorful since I learned to speak the language."

Real understanding starts from "heart"

Asked why he chose to work at Shenzhen Jade Cargo International, he answered, "It was an excellent opportunity for me."

Before that he lived in Germany with his wife for four or five years, working for Lufthansa as a PR manager in the logistics department.

"I was told that a new cargo airline company had been set up in Shenzhen as a joint venture between Lufthansa and Shenzhen Airlines. I was interested in what the job offered. But what I was most interested in was the fact that I would be able to go to China, because I love it and like the life there, and like speaking the language, enjoying the food and studying the culture."

"I was beside myself with joy when I came back again. But my wife didn't feel that way. Years of life in Germany unfitted her for life in China since she was so fond of and had got used to the German way of life."

But he was overjoyed to combine his passion with his work. What's more, Jade Airlines is a new company in a country whose aviation industry is young and burgeoning.

Once he was asked what was the biggest enjoyment he had working at Jade.

"It's an easy question," he turned to his Chinese colleagues, "I have the greatest enjoyment working with them. They are competent, and have broad

Ulrich gives a lecture to his Chinese colleagues.

vision. When I take a business trip somewhere, for example, they tell me a lot of related things, and offer useful suggestions. Of course, I do the same for them. When we combine our knowledge, we finish our job easily, perfectly and happily.

Jade Cargo International, the first of its kind in China, founded in 2005, is a joint venture air freight company. With more than 60 percent of its officers and pilots foreigners, it's a harmonious combination of Eastern and Western cultures. On the occasion of the last Mid-Autumn (Moon) Festival, Ulrich and his Chinese colleagues organized an elaborate party. They invited the new foreign general manager to present moon cakes and other gifts to all the employees, Chinese and foreign. The employees were invited to write down their wishes and sign their names on an autograph board. The whole party liked the East-West conglomeration of celebrations. Through such activities, the foreign employees got to understand the Chinese traditions better, and the Chinese employees got to know their foreign officers better.

"A foreigner feels uncomfortable in an unfamiliar Eastern country if he doesn't speak or read the local language, or doesn't know or get used to local affairs. Quite a few foreigners are dispatched to work in their companies in China, usually as ranking executives, and have to make decisions. How can they be correct in decision-making if they don't understand the country and the mindset of its people well? So I want to act as a bridge of understanding between the two sides in the hope of helping these foreigners and the Chinese get to know each other better and quicker," he said thoughtfully.

Ulrich told us that a couple of years ago he came across an ad which read: Communications start from "heart". He quite agrees with this attention getter. "Some foreigners come to China, but leave the country without

success. I think they have something wrong in their attitude. They tend to believe that China is a very poor country and its people are good for nothing. They are too cocky to communicate with their Chinese employees. Actually, they do not understand the country and do not even speak a single word of Chinese. They are doomed to failure," he added.

To express my mind in Chinese is my goal

He has a happy and joyful life in China because he has a sweet-natured and beautiful wife, two lovely kids and a family full of warmth.

When talking about his romantic date with his wife, his account was brief and humorous. "I was an intern in a company when I came to work here for the first time. Later, my boss opened another company in Jiangsu Province, and engaged me as a technical manager. The company's business expanded so fast that I needed to get more and more hands. Every time we hired a new employee I had to talk it over with the personnel manager. And gradually the personnel manager became my wife. Now we have two children."

His wife is from Jiangsu, a province famous for beautiful ladies. But he has something new to add: "All young ladies in China are attractive, not only in Jiangsu. All Chinese girls are beautiful in my eyes. 'Love me, love my dog.' Maybe it is because I love China that I think all Chinese girls are beautiful."

He went on, "My children speak Chinese as well as German. I am very proud of them. Instead of sending them to an international school which emphasizes English, I sent them to a Chinese school because they can learn

The wall of Ulrich's office is decorated with Chinese artworks.

pure Chinese there. I think English is easier. In terms of cultural profundity, I prefer Chinese for my kids. I hope they will get a complete understanding of China, its people, the Chinese way of good conduct, and its culture in particular."

He has set up such a standard for his children because he has a great interest in Chinese culture and a wide reading spectrum. When he was a teenager, his parents gave him a Chinese picture book. The ancient temples and other buildings and the ingenuous looks of the Chinese people in the book left him with a very deep impression, and roused his aspiration to visit this big country and learn about its ancient culture.

He found that Chinese culture is amazing and extraordinary after reading many of the Chinese classics, like the *Analects of Confucius* and *Sun Tzu's Art of War*. Some say philosophy originated in the East and science in the West. Ulrich is convinced of this.

Ulrich still works hard on his Chinese, even though he speaks it fluently.

His plan is to be able to read newspapers and magazines in Chinese in one year and to write Chinese on his computer in the near future, in a word, to express his ideas and thoughts in the language.

"I admire the Chinese people"

He likes the Chinese people. Ulrich said, "The Chinese people are adaptable, easygoing and considerate to others. Maybe these are the key factors in their success."

Among the great Chinese figures that he admires the most are Mao Zedong and Deng Xiaoping. "Deng is always a topic of conversation among the Shenzhen people," he noted. "He was short, but had the greatest momentum. He was removed from his leading positions three times, and was even sent into exile to a remote area for years. But he bounced back. He made great decisions that have profoundly changed the country. Look at Shenzhen. A small fishing village was turned into a metropolis in a very short period of time. How could the world not be amazed at such a great development?"

Ulrich likes the bustling scene in the morning on Shenzhen's streets. "People here are not necessarily rich, but they look peaceful and free from worries. Look at the trash collector riding his tricycle. The morning sunshine is reflected on his jubilant face. He looks happy, though the work is dirty and hard. It is really marvelous."

Ulrich has observed that everywhere in China you can find that people are full of vigor, vitality and dedication to their work. When they hit upon a good idea, they are encouraged to put it into action. All in all, the Chinese people are enthusiastic and willing to work hard, happily and joyfully. In

Western society, however, many people don't work so hard and still complain a lot, though the government provides them with good welfare services.

"Furthermore, the Chinese people are not only hard working but also modest," he said. "They don't like flaunting, not like the boastful people whom you will easily see through when you come into close contact with them. They are a people of great endurance who bear whatever hardships they encounter. They will start over again if they fail the first time and will go on until they succeed, just like water dripping non-stop day by day, which wears the hardest rock away." He feels great admiration for this spirit.

Ulrich often refers to the catchphrase the Chinese people like most: Be a decent person first, and then act. Indeed, he has learned a lot from the Chinese about how to behave.

By Liu Dongping
Translated by Yang Yaohua
Photos provided by Liu Dongping and Li Yifeng

Personal File

Name: Howard Snyder

Chinese Name: Shi Yingshan

Nationality: American

Occupation: Operations manager for the
Olympic project team of Coca-Cola
(China) Documentary Filmmaker

Time in China: 9 years

A Garrulous American in Beijing

Howard Snyder is a garrulous foreigner and a cross-talk lover. After he finished his studies in China, he was fated to have a permanent relationship with the country. He has traveled in China many times and lived in China for four different times. Due to his Beijing accent, he calls himself a Beijinger and sometimes has a local bias against others. Twelve years ago, he made friends with a group of Chinese children, and this year he came to Beijing specially to search for his old friends. He is operations manager for the Olympic project team of Coca-Cola, but he insisted on being an Olympic volunteer on the street for one day. After he showed up on TV, he got the most votes from the audience in the TV program *Olympic Fan* and has the tendency to be the *No.1 Foreign Olympic Fan*.

$\mathcal{M}$rs Ma, a folk art teacher of the Children's Palace, called *Seven Days*, a program of BTV (Beijing Television Station), saying that a foreigner was trying to search for his old friends with whom he had learned cross-talk 12 years previously, and wondered whether our program could help him find his old classmates. We all thought it was an attractive idea, and considered that we could also help him by getting him to appear on a TV program to improve our audience rating.

His name is Howard Snyder, and he is the operations manager for the Olympic project team of Coca-Cola (China). He took part in the sponsorships for the 2002 FIFA World Cup Korea / Japan, Shanghai Special Olympics, World Expos, Beijing Olympic Games and Paralympics Games, and was in charge of security, crisis management and operations management. Before that he had done some financial jobs and had been a consultant for many Fortune 500 companies, helping them with their China entry strategy. Now he is also a documentary playwright-director, and can't wait to try children's TV programs. His hobby is cross-talk, so his Beijing accent is very authentic and fluent, and he is happy and proud to be garrulous.

Sure enough, our contact with this garrulous guy led to two very popular

TV programs.

Searching for old friends in Beijing

Howard is well built and has two "one hundred and seventies": he is 170 cm tall and weighs 170 *jin* (one jin equals half a kg). He often mocks himself, saying, "I am frequently invited to dinners, and Chinese food is too delicious, so…." Asked how his Chinese name came about, he said, "My family name Snyder is transliterated into the Chinese family name Shi. I worship heroes, so I chose the character Ying (meaning hero), and Shan is easy to spell. It so happens that a mountain with a quartz mine can also be called a Shi Yingshan in Chinese."

On May 31, 1962, Howard was born in Rochester, New York State. "I am 46 years old and I am a tiger." He was mentioning his Chinese zodiac sign, "I am Jewish. My father was a lawyer, and our family could be called upper-middle class." Brought up in the third-biggest city in New York State—Rochester—he received a good education. Why did he come to China to search for his old friends since his ancestors had nothing to do with China? It is a long, long story.

Howard feels elated every time he passes Tiananmen Square.

He is a language genius, and became interested in all kinds of languages when he was young. "I learnt

Spanish first, and then Chinese, Japanese, Vietnamese and Portuguese. I can speak some Thai and Nepali, too. I am Jewish, so I can speak Hebrew, and also I know a little Mongolian, not very good though, just for communication." Apart from his mother tongue, which language he is best at? "I am good at Chinese and Japanese, but my other languages are just so-so." You don't mix up the characters in Chinese and Japanese? "Not really. It is easy for me to read and draw up contracts and documents, and I am very familiar with economic and financial vocabulary. Reading novels is not so easy for me, for I can't sense the subtleties of those literary works."

Is it useful to learn so many languages? "For me, yes. One more language means more friends in one more country. For example, Chinese gives me 1.3 billion new friends. I like to travel, and I hate it most when I go to a country whose language I don't know, for it is embarrassing and frustrating. If I know its language, even a few words, their attitude towards you will be completely different." He is very proud of his Chinese level, "There are four tones in Chinese, and they are hard to master. Chinese characters are very mysterious and rich in connotations. I am proud to learn Chinese characters, and I feel good that I can read them. My Chinese can surprise some Chinese people."

Mentioning why he learnt Chinese, he said, "I am adventurous. China was a very mysterious place when I began to study Chinese in 1980. I thought Europe represented the past while Asia represented the future. The Chinese population accounts for some one fourth of that of the world, so I thought it might be useful to learn Chinese." Before he came to Beijing Normal University, he first spent one year learning Chinese in America, and acquired basic speaking skills but fewer than 1,000 Chinese characters. Then he studied at Beijing Normal University for two semesters—less than a year.

"From 1981 to 1982 I spent six months at Beijing Normal University and four months traveling around the country. I went to Xinjiang, Dunhuang, Harbin, Guilin, Dali, Kunming, Mount Tai, Mount Huang, Xi'an, Suzhou, Shanghai, Chengde, Datong, and many other places."

Right after China's reform and opening-up, a high-nosed and deep-eyed foreigner walking on the street would draw the attention of many, especially children who would follow behind. Of course, Howard couldn't avoid being taken as a different species, either; but indeed he felt like he was on an alien planet. "I was alone, so I had to force myself to speak Chinese. The travelers I met on trains were my Chinese teachers." Howard's Chinese improved very quickly in this flowing linguistic context.

Before he arrived in China, his Chinese teacher introduced him a relative living in Beijing with whom he could practice Chinese. The relative of the teacher was an educated youth returning to Beijing from the countryside. This well experienced guy with a standard Beijing accent lived in a multi-family old courtyard house in Xinjiekou. In the following days Howard frequently went to him for Chinese knowledge. There were many educated youths who had returned to Beijing and had no job yet. In his spare time, Howard often chatted with them, so he had even more free Chinese lessons from these Beijingers. Cracking sunflower seeds, having tea and chatting with those hospitable neighbors was definitely the best way to learn Chinese. In the courtyard, Howard's Chinese improved very quickly, besides, he got to know about the daily life of ordinary Chinese people.

He was impressed very much by his one year's study in China, and especially by the Chinese people's hospitality, passion, diligence and intelligence. That is why he has never forgotten Beijing. "There is a Chinese saying—*ou* what *si lian*? (I gave him a hint: '*ou duan si lian*'). Yeah, *ou duan si lian*, which means separated but still in close spiritual connection. The connection between China and me has never been cut since 1982, and has become part of my life." It is true. He kept China in his heart and returned to China occasionally and stayed here for a month or a week. His longest stay was from late 1989 to 1990.

The center of gravity of his career is in the Orient. He lived in Japan for ten years in all, and certainly can speak Japanese. During the 2002 FIFA World Cup Korea / Japan, Coca-Cola served as the sponsor, and he was the project director. "When I stayed in Japan, Da Shan became famous in China in 1989. Before I knew him I saw many foreigners show up on TV and they talked about some funny things to entertain people, and that was how they made a living. I thought I was a pretty funny man, so I could do that, too. It would be good for a foreigner to be a star in Asia."

From 1995 to late 1997, when Howard worked in Beijing, he found some foreigners appearing on TV in China, and it was due to their cross-talk that they became popular with Chinese audiences. So he went to the Chinese Department of Beijing University to visit Wang Jingshou, who knew cross-talk very well. Mr Wang had been Da Shan's teacher. "Mr Wang recommended me to many people, like Mrs Ma of the Children's Palace and Mr Ding Guangquan, who had cultivated many foreign students. Then Mrs Ma told me that she was teaching a children's cross-talk class. I think it is good to learn foreign languages from children, for they are innocent and always tell the truth, so I began to take cross-talk classes with the children in the Children's Palace."

Those children were surprised and excited to see a foreign uncle step-

ping into the classroom and becoming their classmate, and this uncle was innocent enough to play with them. The children liked this old classmate very much, for he was extremely funny, and he could play with them like a student of their own age. When it came to their cross-talk perform-ance, the foreign adult face set off by a very short child was a funny enough picture itself, but when they added funny dialogues, their performance never failed to make everyone laugh. During that

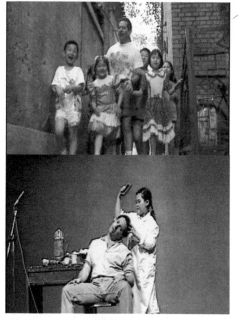

Scenes of ten years ago reappear: running merrily and acting in a play.

period of time, he took advanced classes at the Beijing Film Academy, and made a special film of his cross-talk performances with the children, which was broadcast on Beijing TV.

He took classes at the Children's Palace every Saturday and Sunday for one and a half years. His 34th birthday party was held at a Children's Day ceremony at a school where he performed as a member of the Children's Palace. The children of the school tied a red scarf around his neck, the performance team's young members offered him passionate blessings, and they shared a birthday cake, which left him with an unforgettable beautiful memory. I asked him to comment on the children. He said, "They are from Beijing, very talka-tive, especially during cross-talk performances, very funny and innocent. We soon became familiar with each other, and they accepted me very well. Those friendly young classmates stand for Beijing's traditional alley culture."

In 2003, Howard came back to Beijing to work in finance here, and stayed for two years. His major task was to deal with bad debts. "I was the first foreign Huang Shiren in China." Huang Shiren was the evil landlord who dunned debtors to death in the opera *The White Hair Girl*.

This time, his visit to Beijing made him very thoughtful. "China has changed tremendously. Skyscrapers are everywhere. The economy has improved a lot, and so have people's attitudes. People are all busy now, and some are leading a tiring existence. It is no longer that easy to make friends in China now, for the connections between people are getting looser. This is not unique to China. With the development of the country and the fast economic pace, it is inevitable that people get more and more estranged. That is why I miss the old days. Chinese people are very hospitable, but they are too busy now. It is a contradiction. In the 1980s and 1990s, I often visited Chinese friends in their houses, but it can't happen now. They are too busy to eat at home. I think you can't really know a Chinese person if you haven't visited his house."

He missed the old days, and also missed those friendly young classmates. This is the reason why the American came to Beijing to search for his old friends.

"My Beijing birthday"

With Mrs Ma and the documentaries taken in those days, his search was not a hard one. After we broadcast a notice on TV, the children automatically

contacted us or Mrs Ma. Then we settled when and where the children would meet Howard and Mrs Ma.

Seeing each other again, Howard and the children were all excited and surprised. Howard, the former Uncle Shi, was very surprised too. "Is this the little fellow in my memory? He is taller than me now, and his face has completed changed." The friendly young classmates were surprised: "Uncle Shi used to be very tall and strong, so why he is shorter now?" In those days, they had to look up to see his face, but now even the girls needn't do it, let alone the boys.

Twelve years ago, Howard spent his birthday with these children. Interestingly, his birthday falls May 31, the day before Children's Day, so the children were celebrating Uncle Shi's birthday while celebrating their own holiday at the same time. But this time the children had become young men and big girls clustering around Uncle Shi. They smiled and exulted, as if their childhood had come back again.

Mrs Ma has retired, but she still goes to the Children's Palace to teach children. She doesn't care that she has little monetary compensation. "It is

Uncle Shi is back.

my life, though it brings me not much material profit. I feel satisfied when I teach. In my opinion, it is rare that a person can do his ideal work as a livelihood. Luckily, I like my job. That is enough." She has a deep love for traditional Chinese art forms, and she loves children, so she hopes traditional art forms can take root in the heart of the children and be passed down from generation to generation.

Howard admires Mrs Ma's selfless dedication. Once seeing her, he wanted to give her a warm hug, but was rejected. "Come on. Don't do that. I am not used to it." We all laughed. Mrs Ma is of the same age as our parents. They are like a thermos, warm inside but cold outside. Unlike Howard's friendly young classmates, they are shy to express their love for others. But we still showed this scene for it was very interesting. Sure enough, seeing our program on TV, my parents smiled heartily. When Howard's documentary was being shown, the audience burst into roars of laughter.

We recorded the whole process of his search. On the principle of resource sharing, we made our programs, and he supplemented his documentary which had been taken 12 years previously with this material. Mentioning why he wanted to make a documentary, he said, "I studied 12 years ago at the Beijing Film Academy, and worked at a TV station, so I was fond of media and films. In those days a Japanese TV station once cooperated with Beijing TV. One reason why I learnt cross-talk 12 years ago was that I felt that foreigners knew too little about China. I thought it would be a good way to help them get to know China better if I introduced my experience to them."

But why did he have to do it in 2008? "Because every 12 years forms a cycle by the traditional Chinese calendar. And the Year of the Rat has come round again," he said. "In my opinion, the Rat, the first of the 12 zodiacal

signs, stands for a new start. There is a Chinese idiom—everything renews. From one Rat year to another, everything will change a lot, so I think I should film these children again. I think it is worthwhile to tell foreigners the changes in China through the changes in them. It is almost 30 years since my first arrival in China. I think it is my duty to introduce China to foreign people, for they know so little about China. Besides, this year the Beijing Olympic Games will draw the attention of the world to Beijing and China. I must take this chance to show everything I know about China to foreigners."

What do you think of the search for these kids? "It is a wonderful story, I think. In foreign countries, news about China is always very gloomy or negative. I don't think foreigners know what China really is like. I want to show the real China and those Chinese children to foreigners, to get them to know China better." Howard's angle should be regarded as a good one. A kid changes a lot over 12 years, and so does China. Though very small, his documentary is really good enough to reflect the whole country.

The sight of every child surprised him, but he thought he needn't be surprised. "We all have our own ideas and ambitions; it doesn't matter whether you are a child or an adult. Now some of them want to go abroad, some want to make films, and some want to be teachers. None of this surprises me. It is growth. Twelve years ago they were hard working good kids and well literate. What excites me most is that they didn't just follow the mainstream. They are designing their own life. They are all interested in Beijing and its culture, and have confidence in their future."

It took Howard four months to finish his documentary, which is called "My Beijing Birthday". A man with his zodiacal sign of the Tiger unexpectedly recorded his story of spending his birthdays in two years of the Rat. But of course he wouldn't mix the Tiger with the Rat, as a pop song says, "Rat, Tiger, hard to tell one from the other." Very cunningly, he used his birthdays to introduce the past and future of a group of children and reflect China's changes during the 12 years following the reform and opening-up.

In late June, he showed his documentary at the Cervantes Institute near Chaoyang Park. The documentary was edited and subtitled in English all by himself. It has a fluent transition of the camera and good structure, very nice and professional, and it impressed me, though I am professional. In the documentary there were Tiananmen Square, Chang'an Street, the changes of the cityscape over the previous 12 years, the children 12 years before and now, and, of course, Howard himself, who was very slender 12 years ago but is now plump.

"To make a film is just like the process when a woman gives birth to a baby. I am a man, unable to give birth to a baby, but I am a writer, and this film is as good as my baby. If you have a baby, you definitely want to show it to your friends. It is a very hard and painful process, but with a good result it will make everyone happy."

When the lights were turned on, Howard introduced to the audience the characters in the film—the little children and his teacher Mrs Ma.

The audience's applause brought Howard a sense of achievement. "My work is popular. So I am very happy. Every author hopes his work will be liked by the audience. They were touched, which proves that my love for Beijing is true, not false. They are wise enough to tell true from false. We are all bombarded with information these days. Most of the audience today were foreigners who have lived and worked in Beijing for a long time, and so I am very glad they acknowledged my work."

Only one person was overwhelmed by tears. It was Mrs Ma, who was dominated by her complicated feelings. She suddenly held Howard in her arms, and didn't let go for a long time. The change from her rejection to her volunteer hug surprised me. Once boiling, hot water will spill out of a thermos.

Howard explained Mrs Ma's tears in these words: "Why did she cry? I think that is the exact difference between China and America. Americans are used to expressing their feelings in public, but Chinese are restrained, shy to express their feelings publicly. Seeing her many years' experience of teaching children cross-talk displayed here, she thought of lots of things. It (to cry) was catharsis for her. For example, in America those who took part in the Vietnam War never mention their war experience; your parents' generation doesn't want to talk about the 'cultural revolution', either, though everyone knows about it. Today her work was acknowledged by all, and she got pleasure out of this spiritual catharsis."

In a sobbing voice, Mrs Ma told me: "I am very touched. As an American, he loves Chinese children and traditional Chinese art so much. I am very moved that a foreigner has such a deep love for Chinese art and Chinese children especially in this modern and colorful society. He is the one who loves the children most, and keeps them in mind for 12 years. I want to say thanks to *Seven Days* for helping him and these children realize their dreams. These children have few chances to reunite, for Beijing is so big and they have changed so much."

The characters in the documentary had many feelings, too. We attached importance to the opinion of a young man called Liu Hengjun, for, first, he showed up most frequently in the film and, second, he is also an artistic worker. "How did you feel when you saw yourself as a young boy?" He replied, "It is hard to say whether we were innocent or foolish in those days. Is what I have got enough to compensate for what I have lost? Thinking of this, I get very complicated feelings."

I asked him to comment on Howard. He said: "He is another Norman Bethune (a Canadian who dedicated himself to the Chinese revolution), an international friend. His documentary, I think, has lots of things in common with that of a master (he probably meant Antonioni), for his concern is Chinese people, living people, not simply symbols or politics. That is very good."

"As a director, what do you think of his film?"

"It's very sincere."

Howard plans to send his film to foreign film festivals. He also hopes it could be broadcast by foreign TV stations to let the outside world know more about China.

"I am an Olympic Fan!"

With the Olympic Games approaching, Howard called to ask me for a chance to be a volunteer for a day. I agreed and let him come to take part in our TV program called Olympic Fans. "I am an Olympic fan!" He said immediately.

We took him to Gui Street, which is famous for its special snacks. He could serve there as a guide for pedestrians. He put on a volunteers T-shirt, and began work.

The volunteers there gave him a job test first by asking him the origin of Gui Street. Very calmly, he began his introduction: "The Gui as in Gui Street is not the same as the word Gui (the two words are homonyms, and the latter means ghost). Gui (the former Gui) is used in sacrificial rituals as a container for meat as sacrifice to the Gods. In the old days there were many coffin

stores on this street, so it was called Gui (the latter Gui) Street, and later it was renamed Gui (the former Gui) Street for auspiciousness." A volunteer told him another explanation, "Maybe in the Qing Dynasty (1644-1911) there was a night market here which opened after twelve o'clock at night. When it opened, the owners of the many coffin stores would light candles. Seen from afar the candles were like ghostly fires. That is why everyone called it Gui (the latter Gui) Market."

Immediately Howard asked, "Where are you from?" The reply was "Hebei Province". Howard then asked the others: "Look, he is from Hebei, and I am from Beijing. Who is right?" All the volunteers laughed. "I came to Beijing in 1981. Which of you were born before that? Hands up. See? I have stayed longer in Beijing than they have, so I am senior enough to test them first. Call me brother, if you don't call me uncle. Ha-ha."

Once he began his work he became a very qualified guide. Besides giving directions to pedestrians, he introduced the various special snacks on Gui Street to them. If someone wanted to go to the airport, he would ask about their budget (he deserves to be called a financial expert), and then he would tell him which route and bus could save him money. Maybe because a foreign guide was seldom seen, many pedestrians came to him for directions, and of course some of them wanted to test his knowledge of Beijing.

A little child from Guangdong who was visiting Beijing greeted Howard with the phrase "Welcome to Beijing". Howard immediately used Cantonese to greet the little visitor, and said "I am a Beijinger, so I should say to you 'Welcome to Beijing'." Howard really has the spirit of being a good host.

His was not satisfied with giving directions only. Soon he became interested in a trishaw. He struck up a conversation with the driver, asking the latter to pretend to be a traveler and sit on the trishaw. Then this foreign volunteer was seen driving a Chinese around different alleys and introducing to him the scenic spots along the way. When they were finished, we asked the driver to grade Howard, and he gave him eighty

As a volunteer for the 2008 Olympic Games, Howard makes his own contribution by giving directions to a child.

percent. However, Howard was not convinced by this grade: "I am a Beijinger, and you are from Henan. Your Beijing accent is not as standard as mine." The same thing was happening again. He insisted that he was a Beijinger, and sometimes he had local prejudice towards others.

It was hot, and pedaling a trishaw was very exhausting. Soon Howard was bathed in sweat. I kidded him that he could take this chance to lose weight. He said, "I eat too much in China. After the Olympics, I will lose

ten kg. If Director Yang is not satisfied, I will lose 15." Certainly I supported him. "What about making another program when I get thinner?" he suggested.

Deal!

From August 8 he became very busy. We

Experiencing the lives of a rickshaw man and tourist guide.

couldn't reach him by phone, maybe because he was shuttling among different stadiums. Phone signals are not good in the Bird's Nest and Water Cube. Plus, the cheering audience was a barrier between us. Well, we can ask him about his Olympic experience after the Olympics and Paralympics.

Now he was no longer a mere Olympic fan, but director of the Olympic projects of Coca-Cola, one of the sponsors of the Games.

"I am a Beijinger"

I asked him: "Which country do you prefer, America or China?" He replied, "Let me put it this way. I will never forget I am American and Jewish. America is my birthplace, so I love it, certainly. Meanwhile, I am a Beijinger. I came to China in 1981, and since then China has become part of my life. I have kept developing myself as China is carrying out her reform and opening-up. After the Olympics, China will continue her development, and I will develop, too, of course in China. My love for her is beyond words. Both my motherland and China are part of my life, no matter whether I am happy or upset, willing or unwilling. China will be part of my life till I am dead. Yes, I love both America and China, but in different ways.

He never regards himself as a foreigner, so he is not used to some young people's blind worship of foreign countries. For example, a Chinese girl with a foreign name, Jodie, was unhappy when Howard addressed her using her Chinese name. Then Howard became unhappy, too. He said, "Is your Chinese name no good or something? " I said, "You have a Chinese name, so why don't you allow others to have foreign names? Isn't it a double standard?" He countered, "That is different. If you live in America, to have an American name is good for your work and life, and to get close to others. But why must you be Jodie and let people mistake you for a foreigner since you live in China? It doesn't make any sense. I can't understand it."

I am not a paparazzi, but sometimes I like gossip. I asked about his marital status. He said he was not married yet, but had once been in love in Japan. "I didn't marry a Japanese girl, though a near miss." Recently he had just finished a relationship in China, too. "And I didn't marry a Chinese girl, either." I asked what his ideal woman was like, he said, "I am doomed to live and work in the Orient, so I don't want a Western girl without an Oriental background. Definitely I will find a girl here. I hope she will be smart and independent. It would be better if she liked sports, and was optimistic, cheerful and a little fleshy." It seems he doesn't like skinny beauties. Don't lose too much weight, girls!

I asked him about his future plans. He said first he would take his film to foreign film festivals, TV stations and American universities to tell the world what China is really like; second he would work on children's TV programs in China; and third he would like to build an international school to let children learn and grow up there happily. Besides, he said, his experience in many of the world's top 500 companies and his good connections in China will probably bring him great achievements if he works in China for foreign companies as a counselor. He loves a free life style and free work style.

Good luck to this Beijinger!

By Yang Weisi
Translated by Zhang Ruiqing

Personal File

Name: Eunice Moe Brock

Chinese Name: Mu Lin'ai

Nationality: American

Occupation: "Philanthropy Ambassador"

Time in China: 22 years

Pursuer of Childhood Dreams

Eunice Moe Brock (Mu Lin'ai in Chinese) looks like a typical American woman. But at the age of 82 she sold all her property, including land, house and car, bade farewell to her family, and traveled all the way across the Pacific Ocean to China. She decided to settle down and spend the rest of her life in a small village in China's Shandong Province.

Eunice wishes to be granted a "green card" to live in the country permanently. She has decided in her will to donate her remains to science. "Everyone has his or her feelings of life that can not be fully understood by others," she said regarding her decision.

"My 90th birthday is coming. I am so happy to see the newborn babies today." On the morning of July 10, 2007, Eunice made the rounds of the maternity wards at Liaocheng International Peace Hospital, of which she is the honorary president. There she celebrated her 90th birthday by ushering new lives into the world.

In Liumiao, a small village in Yanggu County in Shandong, almost all the seniors have received blessings from Eunice and all the children have enjoyed the lovely toys at her home. If you ask the villagers if there is a foreigner in their village, maybe they won't know how to answer. But if you mention the name of Mu Lin'ai (Eunice Moe Brock), they will surely lead you to her home. They will tell you Eunice is regarded as a senior member of their families. She hails the village folks she meets in the streets by saying in Chinese: "Have you had your meal yet?" a typical Chinese greeting to friends.

Grow up and come back to China

Nine years have elapsed since Eunice settled in Liumiao Village.

Her strong attachment to China dates back to the beginning of the last

century. In 1902, Eunice's parents came to China as Christian missionaries, and gave birth to her in 1917, the fourth of their five children.

She lived in the Liaocheng area of Shandong Province until she returned to the US with her parents at the age of 13. The old China in her memory was scourged by war, poverty, plague and all other suffering you could name. She saw with her own eyes ragged beggars, children swapped for food, roadside deaths from cold and starvation. "Can I do something for them?" she kept asking her mother. "You are too young," her mother would say. "Come back and do something for them when you grow up."

"Grow up and come back to China" was a long-cherished wish in her mind.

She had a childhood playmate, Zhou Renjie, when she was in Liaocheng. Eunice had been out of contact with him since she went back to her home country. But she has still kept a picture taken with Zhou.

In a letter she wrote in 1992 to the municipal government of Liaocheng, Eunice detailed her childhood experience in China and her wish to live in the country as a permanent resident. She also asked the local authorities to inquire about her childhood friend Zhou Renjie. The city government took the matter very seriously, and went to a lot of trouble to find Zhou's children. Baoluo, Zhou's first son, who worked at a hospital attached to the Shandong petrochemical industry, immediately wrote to her: "I feel both happy and sad reading your letter. I am happy, because my father's childhood friend is still living a healthy life and still remembers him and his family; I feel sad, because my father died of a cerebral hemorrhage at the early age of 49 in 1964. When I was a child, my grandma and father told me they often got a lot of assistance from your family. Yours was the kindest family in the world, they said, and your affection for them was more valuable than gold. My father was conservative, honest and kind. He made a living as a clock repairer, and raised seven children. He treasured his friendship with you, and, to commemorate it, gave me a foreign name, Baoluo (Paul)…."

Eunice was deeply touched by the transnational friendship her childhood playmate had treasured so dearly. Three months later, Eunice came to China on a trip with her husband. In Liaocheng, the couple met Paul and Zhou's other children, and got a splendid, heartfelt welcome. They toured the city of Liaocheng together with Zhou's family. On the return to her childhood home which has seen earthshaking changes, Eunice was all aflame with excitement. After two weeks in Liaocheng, the couple visited Guilin, the Three Georges, Tibet, and other places. During the tour of nearly two months, Eunice saw the great changes that had taken place in China. The tour deepened her understanding of the country, and furthered her determination to live here when the right chance came in the future.

In 1998, her beloved husband passed away. The indescribable loneliness made her long even more for those simple, kindhearted people in the faraway country. The loneliness and the strong desire accelerated her decision to live in China. Regardless of discouragement by her children, the carefree Eunice sold her 40 acres of land, house, car, and all her other property, made light of traveling thousands of miles across the Pacific Ocean, and settled down as a new member in Liumiao Village, where she had spent years as a child.

Many people wonder what brought Eunice to China. "I was born in China, and grew up in China. I am an American, but I have a Chinese heart," she said.

American granny's life in China

A blonde foreign granny's unexpected coming to the small quiet village stirred great curiosity amongst the local folks. But Eunice soon gained their respect and love.

The local people like to drop in at the affable American granny's home. At holiday time, the villagers pay visits to her, and extend to her their sincere greetings in different ways.

Her house is an ordinary one, typical of North China's rural areas. When she first applied for residence in Liaocheng, according to the villagers, Eunice asked to live in a village with the harshest conditions. Considering that her advanced age would cause her many inconveniences in a poor village, the local government "misleadingly" told her that Liumiao was the poorest. The village committee and the other folks of Liumiao vacated the best house they had for her. They furnished the house with a fridge, a color TV, a telephone, a sofa, and a lot of other appliances and furniture. "I am here to take root here, not to be a guest," she told the folks who greeted her. "I will feel uneasy and guilty if I give you too much trouble."

Since she lived in the US for nearly 70 years, she has almost forgotten all her Chinese. So the village hired a female interpreter specifically for her. She was deeply appreciative of their consideration. She insisted on paying for the furniture and appliances. And she was adamant that she should pay for the electric power and the interpreter service, and didn't want to burden the village with any extra expense.

Local villagers come to celebrate her birthday on August 11 every year.

Upon hearing the news that an American granny had come, the village kids burned with curiosity, and rushed to see her. The granny loves these kids, and the kids love her, too. With a great variety of toys in the sitting room, her home is a gathering place for the kids. "My home is your home, so come whenever you want," she says in her halting Chinese when kids visit her. In order to give the kids the most fun she could, she sent people to buy toy building blocks, badminton sets, comic strips, children's English readers, and many more. The children play joyfully to their heart's content at granny's home. Sometimes she plays badminton and read picture books with the kids; sometimes she pieces toy blocks together into English words to teach them.

August 11 is her birthday. On this day very year, the village kids present her with a birthday cake; village grandmas come with birthday greetings and hold her hands, chatting. The happy Eunice shares the cake with her visitors. Then an evening birthday party is held at the Liaocheng International Peace Hospital.

Every year Eunice has two parties on the same day to celebrate her

birthday.

In the summer of 2008, four students from the Chengdu Academy of Music shot a documentary on her life. Knowing Eunice's birthday was coming, the students held a special birthday party in her honor ahead of time. Sitting on a sofa, hand in hand with two old friends she had invited to the party, Eunice said, "I feel a special love, special warmth at this moment."

The Christmas of 1999 was the first one she spent in China. Christmas trees were not available in the local area, so the village committee specially sent people to Shanghai for one. She had a delightful Christmas with the village kids. On the occasions of Chinese New Year and the Moon Festival, the villagers vie with one another to invite Eunice to their homes, or deliver dumplings and mooncakes to her home.

Dressed up like "Santa Claus", Eunice took a small donkey cart loaded with Christmas gifts to school just before Christmas in 2000.

Eunice finds a tricycle convenient for getting around the village.

On the eve of Christmas 2000, Eunice took a special trip to the county town, and bought more than 100 kg of candies and fancy custom-made candy bags with "Merry Christmas" printed on them. She divided the candies into 800 bags. On the early morning of Christmas Day, Eunice groomed the donkey the village committee had given her, decorated the animal with a red bow on its head, and loaded the gift candy bags onto a cart. On her way to the village school, the villagers standing on both sides of the street gave her a big round of applause, and followed her to the school.

In 1998, soon after she had arrived in Liumiao Village, the local folk were very curious about her, thinking this American granny wouldn't stay long but would escape from the harsh conditions there and go back to the United States. So they had a sort of lukewarm attitude to her. But very soon she gained the respect and love of the people of Liumiao and other villages nearby.

To make it easier to move about in the village, Eunice bought a tricycle in her first year. She would ride it to her greenhouse, or to visit neighbors. Eight years have passed, and the tricycle is covered with rust. Nevertheless,

she is reluctant to change it for a new one.

Planting flowers

Now, the granny has got used to Chinese farmers' life. She grows vegetables herself, and has turned an abandoned lot into a big flower garden. Last fall, she built a green-house in the garden, using an electric saw and a power drill herself. Her home is a cosy one: Hung up on one wall inside the blue-brick and green-tile house is an oil painting she did when she was in her early eighties; just outside one window is a rockery she designed with an artificial waterfall. In Liumiao Village, people call her "Inventor Granny".

"It's a pity that I didn't keep speaking Chinese after I returned to the US," she says with regret. "My spoken Chinese is no more than some simple words, like 'Ni Hao' (hello) and 'Xie Xie' (thank you). I wouldn't have to talk with my fellow villagers with body language if I spoke a little better."

Having experienced China's tremendous changes

"I have experienced the tremendous changes which have taken place in China," Eunice told her family back in the US in one of the more than 100 letters she has written in the last eight years.

She always has a stirring of emotion when mentioning the great changes in the rural area especially.

In her childhood memories, the rural tracks were muddy and made the going very hard. Now they have been replaced with beautiful wide roads paved with concrete. "The paved streets in Liumiao Village have been widened; the main street has been lined on both sides with bushes and trees," she told her family in her first letter.

In 2002, the granny donated a computer lab at the cost of US $30,000 to the village's elementary school. But frequent power failures made it impossible for it to function properly. Two months later, the local government invested almost half a million US dollars in upgrading the power supply and in setting up a DSL service. Since then the computers have been working perfectly, and she has been using email instead of regular letters. "I am happy to have a reliable power supply now; I am even happier that I will not lose any data from my computer any more because there won't be any more power disruptions," she said in an email message. "I think the same is true of other villages. The Chinese government has made great efforts to improve the rural infrastructure to help the needy farmers."

Her neighbor Grandma Zhang told Eunice that she had got the first reimbursement for her medical expense from the government. And Eunice told her American friends in a letter: "A friend told me the villagers have got their cooperative medical insurance service in May at an annual expense of only ten yuan (less than U.S. $1.50) per person. The government will pay half their medical expense. I am delighted with this great leap forward in the medical service."

Not only in the medical service. The government also provides free education to children of farmers, who are the grass-roots of society, she continued in the letter. And she told friends she has been very happy to see and experience, together with her fellow-villagers, the various changes brought about by the high-speed development in China in recent years.

According to the head of the village's women's committee, every year Liumiao Village will give each villager older than 70 a suit of clothes, five pounds of meat and ten pounds of cooking oil at the Chinese New Year. They have free physical checkups every year. Of course Eunice is one of the beneficiaries. On important occasions, the granny always puts on the new clothes the village has custom-made for her.

In 2005, Eunice paid a visit to her family in the US, where she was invited to talk to her church members. She emotionally described the heart-felt treatment she had received in China, and the great many changes that had taken place in the country. Her audience was deeply interested in her one-hour-long speech. After the speech, the church members wouldn't let her go, but asked her many questions for another hour.

Donating her remains to China to fulfill her "dreams"

"I love the Chinese people and I want to do something for them." That's something that always remains in her mind.

Displayed in her office are certificates to titles of "China's Philanthropy Ambassador" and "Shandong Philanthropy Ambassador". When asked about the stories behind them, she always dismisses the question.

Before coming to China, Eunice wished to build a Hope school in the country.

Through the China Youth Development Foundation, Eunice donated 250,000 yuan to purchase computers and sport jerseys for Yucai Elementary School in Liumiao, and build new offices for teachers. Every Chinese New Year she gives some subsidies and gifts to the teachers. Out of gratitude to the American granny, Yucai School has been renamed the China-American Friendship School. At the end of 1999 Eunice was invited to be the honorary principal of the school.

In 2006, Eunice introduced an instrument for students to mitigate stress in their study and to get rid of their nervousness in exams. It is helpful for the village kids to study in a more scientific way. "This instrument is good for medical problems caused by the ever-growing psychological stress suffered by the modern people," she said.

In addition to assistance in kind, Eunice has taken it as a part of her job to promote information exchanges between local schools and the outside world. English teachers from her township often come for "free training" at her home; and thus their English has greatly improved. She has subscribed to foreign magazines on education, and has conducted a study on "how to let kids be successful". She contacts her friends abroad by email almost every day in order to find out their views on education. She also keeps them abreast of the changes taking place in China's rural education. She passes her research findings to the local schools.

The local government and people bear in mind the contributions made by Eunice to their educational undertakings. Just before Teachers' Day in 2002, Anle Township in Yanggu County honored her as an "Exemplary Individual Respecting Teachers and Valuing Education". She said, "It was beyond

my expectation to get a prize in China," when she received the red certificate of the award.

"The granny is very kindhearted," the village committee secretary, Liu Qing'an, told us, "She always does her best to help whoever comes to her, whether she is acquainted with them or not. A deaf-mute woman in our village is good at knitting sweaters. Granny Mu (Eunice) wanted very much to help the woman with financial assistance, but was afraid of hurting her self-esteem; instead, she bought sweaters from her, paying more than ten times the actual price. Also, there was a young sluggard whom all the villagers loathed. But, when she found the young man was fond of music, the granny gave him her electronic keyboard to encourage him to learn a trade and get a job."

In Liumiao Village, you will see fragrant flowers blossoming in everyone's courtyard; and pomegranate, persimmon, pear, and other fruit trees lining both sides of the streets. "The American granny has played a leading role in the landscaping of our village," Yu Huaiqing, a villager, said. "She bought saplings and flower seeds for the villagers. There was a three-acre deserted lot in the village, which she turned into a flower garden by planting more than a dozen kinds of flowers in it."

In a physical checkup several years ago, 23 seniors were diagnosed with cataracts. In 2004, Eunice paid for operations

As one of "the Top Ten Figures who Touched Shandong in 2006", Eunice received a trophy and a prize certificate.

for five of these old patients. "In fact, I wanted to help more people. But my monthly retirement pension of 2,000 US dollars has its limitation. Anyway, I'll help others regain their eyesight when chances come in the future," she said.

In 2003, Eunice made a donation through a charitable organization for the fight against SARS. In 2005, she donated money to Liaocheng Charitable Institution for the tsunami victims in Indonesia. In June 2006, she was invited to the 2006 Conference on the Development of China's Public Welfare Undertakings held in the Great Hall of the People in Beijing. During this conference, Eunice was honored with the title of "China's Philanthropy Ambassador".

On January 11, 2007, Eunice was chosen as one of "the Top Ten Figures who Touched Shandong in 2006". At the award ceremony, she only accepted the trophy cup and the prize certificate, but declined the prize money. Her interpreter Miss Wang Yuqing told us that she was surprised at the money. "Why give me the money? I am here to help, not to be helped." Some of the prize winners were really in need of financial aid, and the money was earmarked for them; and the sponsors awarded the money prize to show their respect, she was told. Knowing that, the kindhearted American granny made a decision that touched all present at the function once again: "I don't need the money. I want to give it to the people who really need it."

"Granny relies on her retirement pension and leads a very simple and frugal life," the interpreter said. "But she is enthusiastic about charitable and public welfare activities. Nobody knows how much she has donated in the past few years." But to the granny, it is nothing important: "I only hope that after a number of years people will still remember an old American lady used to live here. It's of no significance as to what she has done."

The granny has a higher education and a wide range of interests. She wants very much to make contributions to the Chinese people with her knowledge. That's why she wants to stay in this country to continue her service to the Chinese people.

Eunice likes writing. She gets up at four in the morning to write. Not long ago, in a letter to the Organizing Committee for the Beijing 2008 Olympic Games, she made suggestions for its closing ceremony. The letter was published in *China Daily*.

Talking about the letter, the granny emphasized what she was saying by waving her hands: "At the closing ceremony, we should ring big bells and play Tibetan flutes; people from all over the world should sing together 'One World, One Dream'; fireworks should be replaced with music; and let more people be moved and affected."

The high-spirited Eunice recited a poem she wrote for the Olympic Games:

Above the battle cries of war,

Above the hate of race and clan,

We raise the banner of one world,

We wake from lethargy each man,

To use the power of his love,

To make our dream come true,

To use his skills for all mankind,

Working to build the world anew.

"I have already taken part in the Games, though I won't be able to go to Beijing in person," she said.

Attached to her passport is a small card—a volunteer organ donation certificate.

It's a good reminder to attach it to the passport. "Maybe I am too old to donate my organs, but my cornea can be used to help someone recover his or her eyesight. My remains can be used as specimens for scientific research. Ship my remains to the place where it is needed and I'll pay for the shipment. All this is written in my will."

She also expressed her wishes in Chinese: "I want to have a Chinese 'green card', so that I can always live here." She has to go back to the States once a year for a Chinese visa. The arduous trip makes her exhausted. "I just don't want to go back. I have so many things to do here. I have decided to donate my remains to the Chinese health care industry, and I have nothing to worry about in the States. With a 'green card' I will be exempted from the wearying journeys, and will save money from these trips for charitable causes."

We sincerely hope that she will fulfill her long-cherished wishes at an early date.

By Wang Jianzhu
Transalted by Yang Yaohua

Personal File

Name: Paul White

Nationality: British

Occupation: Translator, senior editor

Time in China: 24 years

Living by the Pen for 24 Years

He is seemingly taciturn and serious, a false appearance misleading people who don't know him well. In fact, this foreigner is an erudite scholar of Chinese culture. He has been in China for 24 years at a stretch, living by his pen. He has been amazed and inspired by the great changes he has witnessed, and has ever since stayed on in this culturally fertile Oriental land. He is Paul White, an honest, sincere, and sort of bookish Englishman.

$\mathcal{P}$aul White has been living in China for 24 solid years. He rides a bike to work, instead of driving; he doesn't care for eating out but cooks meals in his own kitchen; he lives alone, with a roomful of books and two computers, one for writing, one for Internet surfing.

His life looks clearly simple, just like a cup of crystal-clear water. We know that people living by the pen, in fact, are more or less the same: myriads of kaleidoscopic phenomena of social life stream out from their pen nibs like mountain springs, or like colorful balloons floating in the air to no-one-knows where.

Coming to China with a pen

In 1984, Paul White came to China at the age of 41, engaged as an expert by Xinhua News Agency. Prior to that, he had worked at the Hong Kong Standard and Trade Media for five years. As a member of the Hong Kong Journalists Association, he organized a group of Hong Kong journalists, the first of its kind, to visit China's mainland in 1982.

Maybe because of this established relation, Paul White came to the news

agency without a hitch, and started working as an English polisher. Paul, in his own words, is an extremely rigorous and meticulous news writer. At first, out of his element in terms of Chinese, he had to frequently consult with his Chinese colleagues about the meaning of Chinese manuscripts. He strives for perfection to ensure the translation is true to the original. As time goes by, his Chinese has constantly improved, which enables him to read voluminous, original books. With his improved Chinese, like adding wings to a tiger, Paul conducts his work more efficiently.

"In order to do a better job, I had to master Chinese," he said, "Only with a mastery of the language was I able to correctly understand the true meaning of the original and to render it into a first-rate work of translation."

It's amazing that Paul reads voluminous Chinese books and even understands obscure classical Chinese prose, but his oral Chinese is still lacking.

Paul never stops working on books.

It seems that, through years' of reading and desk work, Paul has got a good command of a unique secret—"dumb Chinese".

With spring succeeding winter and swallows coming and going, 12 years had elapsed since he came to the news agency. The numerous articles and manuscripts he polished had spread to all parts of the world. As a matter of course, Paul, with a profound knowledge of Chinese as well as English, was transferred to the China Foreign Languages Press as an English expert in charge of correcting and polishing a great amount of important national documents and information for foreign readers.

He has worked for another 12 years at the Press. During this period, he has worked on countless white papers by the Chinese Government, such as *China's Progress in Human Rights in 2004*, *National Minorities Policies and Practice in China*, *Construction of Democratic Politics in China*, *China's Environmental Protection* and *New Progress in China's Protection of Intellectual Property Rights*. The English versions he revised and polished have not only accurately expressed the meaning of the original, but also expressed the accurate meaning in graceful and smooth English to the taste of foreign readers. He has made important contributions to introducing China's social progress and development to the outside world.

In addition, Paul has collated and embellished many English versions of books on ancient Chinese history and philosophy, like *An Outline History of China*, *A History of Chinese Educational Thought*, *A List of Books on Tibetology*, *Confucius*, *Zhuang Zi*, and *Lao Zi*. The list is long. Gradually, Chinese culture and philosophy have seemingly and imperceptibly influenced his life, which can be conjured up from his simple, refined life in harmony with his surrounding world.

He believes his understanding of Chinese society gets deeper every time he finishes work on a book. During the literary work which embodies his painstaking efforts, Paul has grasped the essence of all aspects of the country through reading widely: politics, economy, environmental protection, education, philosophy, history, minority ethnic groups, and traditional medicine. Eventually, he has become a sinologist.

"As a sinologist, you should know everything about the country. I am still learning," Paul said modestly.

Depicting China with his pen

He is very humble about his achievements, but he couldn't hold back his pride when I opened his bookcase.

The first book I noticed was a copy of the bilingual version of *Madame White Snake*, published by the New World Press in the 1990s. "Was it translated all by yourself?" I asked.

"Certainly. This one and these, all translated by myself," he pointed at the rows of books in English: *The Peacock Flies Southeast, Zhao the Orphan, Golden Boy and*

Some of Paul's translation works

Jade Maiden, Autumn in the Han Palace, Snow in Summer, etc. These lively and colorful legends of Chinese traditional culture have turned into lines of English prose, emanating a strong scent of classical culture. Who can tell how many readers in other parts of the world have embellished their dreams with these vivid stories?

"I have to fully understand the meaning of the Chinese original when translating," Paul told me, pointing to a Chinese-English bilingual paragraph in *Madame White Snake*. "I won't do it verbatim into unnatural English, but, in order for my readers to really enjoy the charm of Chinese literature, I strive to convey the subtle artistic conception and aesthetic effects of the original."

From these works of translation, we can see that Paul has a strong interest in ancient Chinese literature. He likes the Han Dynasty the most. "I think China entered into an embryonic stage of civilized modern society in the Han Dynasty, which ushered in the outset of a great civilization. Before that, Chinese history was still primitive with social elements of antiquity."

Besides ancient Chinese literature, Paul has a wide reading and studying spectrum of Chinese medicine and *wushu*. He took part in the work to standardize the translation of traditional Chinese medicine terms into English. The work was highly praised by the related WTO department. He took on the formidable task of correcting and polishing the English translation of the *Compendium of Materia Medica*, a Ming Dynasty work which is regarded as the most complete and comprehensive medical book written in China. Within the short period of only one year, he finished a workload of more than two million words (Usually the annual amount of work is one million words for an expert). His great efforts ensured the timely launch of the English version of this magnum opus and showed the world the cultural gem of Chinese medicine.

Observing with his eyes

Paul reads China with his eyes.

He visited China in 1979 and 1981. The situation in the newly opened China drew his keen attention. He has been amazed and inspired by the great changes he has witnessed in this country during the period from 1984 to 2008.

"It was rather a strange land to me when I saw it for the first time. At that time, China had just embarked on its Four Modernizations program, and the people were poor on the whole. I came to Beijing and found it quite windy and sandy. People protected their TV sets from airborne dust with fabric covers. You would see a thick layer of dust on your desk and window sill every morning when you got up," he recalled the Beijing of the eighties in his vivid, fresh memory.

As a foreign visitor, he has deep impressions of the changes in this country. "The changes have been the most obvious since the beginning of the 1990s. Change. Change. Change. Everything has been changing. Entry into the WTO; the national soccer team qualifying for the World Cup games; first astronaut; and the coming hosting by Beijing of the 2008 Olympics and by Shanghai of the 2010 World Expo. China has experienced unprecedentedly great changes within a period of only ten years."

"The most remarkable changes have taken place in people's living conditions and the environment," Paul told this reporter. "Now, Beijing's climate is much better. Air pollution is not as serious as it used to be. It hasn't been sandy for quite a while." Hiking is his favorite hobby. Whenever he is free at the weekend, he goes with a club called the Beijing Hikers to explore the mountainous regions to the north, northeast and west of Beijing.

He has seen notable changes during his excursions in the countryside. "Farmers are getting richer. There are many restaurants and hostels in the countryside nowadays. And traffic has improved a lot. Ten years ago, we had to come back home the same day when we went hiking, because it was impossible to find a place for the night in the rural areas. Country roads were terrible. Everything is quite different now."

As a writer, he writes whatever he sees worth writing.

Since 1988, he has been writing the "China Diary" column of the *Morning Star*, a newspaper published in London. In the column, he shares his Chinese experiences and viewpoints with his English readers, unfolding a different China in front of the eyes of more and more English readers.

He became enthusiastic when talking about his column: "I write about China's involvement in international politics, its social economics, daily anecdotes, current events, trendy persons, etc. In China, new things are constantly emerging. You have plenty of source materials and always have something to write about."

"I describe the social phenomena I observe in China with a placid mind; not like some reporters, who have only a scanty knowledge of the country, and observe it with preconceived bias and misunderstanding. Their descriptions of China are not objective and factual. I have seen the profound changes in China over many years, and I would say that 90 percent of them are positive. Therefore, the China that flows from my pen is full of vitality."

Loving China with his heart

Paul has accompanied China's march forward for 24 springs and autumns. He just pays one short visit back to the UK a year. China has become his second homeland, one which he cannot be apart from any more.

In 2007, he won a "Friendship Award" for his outstanding contributions to China's foreign publishing undertakings. This is the highest prize given by the Chinese Government to foreign experts working in China.

Paul took out the prize medal from a drawer when talking about the award. He blithely put the medal round his neck, and showed it to me. The usually sedate Paul, now looking like a small kid holding a lollipop, asked me: "Isn't it gorgeous? This is the only prize I have received in China. Of course, it is the only one I have ever had."

He has witnessed people coming and going during all these years at Xinhua and the Foreign Languages Press, Paul told this reporter. Now he is a "veteran" who has the longest seniority among the foreign experts working there. There are so many experts from different countries speaking different languages. They have left their countries to work permanently in China, mainly because they have great attachment to it.

"Paul is an earnest and hardworking expert," Mr. He, director of the English Department of the Foreign Languages Press, commented. "Sometimes, when we have urgent documents to be translated at the weekend, he will work extra hours at home. He is definitely dedicated to his work, and never makes excuses to avoid tasks."

Then how does he get along with his colleagues? Mr. He told this reporter an interesting anecdote: Not long ago, on the occasion of the Spring Festival gala, the performance was over. While everybody was enjoying dishes and drinks, Paul took out a harmonica and gave an impromptu rendition of "The East Is Red." All his colleagues were tickled pink. And his playing of the Chinese folk song "Nan Ni Valley" and the Russian melody "Evenings in Moscow" brought the gala atmosphere to its climax.

"Paul has a very strong attachment to China. He has worked and lived here for such a long time that he has already become a member of our family," Mr He said. "The longer he stays, the more dearly we love each other. Therefore, we hope never to bid him farewell."

By Long Weiwei
Translated by Yang Yaohua

Personal File

Name: Masayo Imura

Nationality: Japanese

Occupation: Head coach

Time in China: 2 years

Japanese Coach in Chinese Team Jersey

She was awarded gold medals twice at Japan's National Synchronized Swimming Championships; she won a prize at the Munich Olympic Games at the age of 22; she started coaching the Japanese national team when she was 28; her team won four silver and four bronze Olympic medals in the 26 years of her coaching life; she is nicknamed "the godmother" and "demon coach". and she led the Chinese Women's National Synchronized Swimming Team to Olympic glory. She is Head Coach Masayo Imura.

*I*n January 2007 leading Japanese coach Masayo Imura signed a contract with China's General Administration of Sports to spearhead the country's national synchronized swimming team, the only female foreign head coach in the Chinese Olympic delegation. Two months after officially assuming the position, Imura led the Chinese team to Melbourne, Australia, for the FINA World Aquatics Championships. On March 17, the first day of the competition, the head coach confidently told Chinese reporters: "I can help the team make history. Now is the first day of this history. The Chinese girls have the ability to catch up with the Japanese and other world-class teams. But they don't know how to. I will guide them. They are so charming that the world will see their improved skills and their great potential. I believe China will be the center of world sports because of the coming Olympics and because of me."

History changed in Melbourne

At the Melbourne World Championships, the Chinese twin sisters Jiang Wenwen and Jiang Tingting, accompanied by the soft melody of "Vagabond

Angel", raised their team to be one of the world's top four in the duet free technical routine. It was their first solid step towards bigger success. The Chinese team, competing with the world's top athletes of the world, got fourth place in the team technical routine. It was their best result so far. Their previous best was only sixth. The importance of the elevation should not be depreciated, though it was only a two-place rise. First, it was the result of team efforts. Second, it was achieved in such a situation that the synchronized performance was scored by judges whose deep-rooted bias was not easy to change. To them, China was not a first-class synchronized swimming country. However, the Chinese team edged out its rivals from the USA, Canada and France, and got closer to the super-class teams from Russia, Spain and Japan. It reflected the progress made by the Chinese team.

The Chinese girls had already laid a certain groundwork for their performance with help from their Chinese instructors. But the progress should also be credited to Masayo Imura, despite the fact that she had been coaching the team for only two months. In the days in Melbourne, Imura, wearing a sports jersey with "China" imprinted on it, always stayed with her team, from training starting at 5 a.m. to contests ending at 8:30 p.m. She had to give interviews to local TV stations, Chinese reporters and Japanese news media.

Imura talks to reporters.

Imura became a focal point during the world championships. As the only foreigner of the 176-member delegation, she gradually integrated herself into the Chinese atmosphere with Chinese athletes, instructors and news reporters.

Her 40-year career has earned her the honor of "godmother"

Imura is a known-to-all prominent figure in Japan's swimming circles. After synchronized swimming became an official sport at the Los Angeles Olympics in1984, the legendary Imura coached the Japanese team for six Olympic Games in a row, and helped them win four silvers and four bronzes. Takeda Miho and Tachibana Miya from her team won a silver medal in the duet event at the 2000 Sydney Olympics, and the same duet received a silver at the 2004 Athens Olympics. In the 2001 Word Aquatics Championships, the duet won first place, the only first achieved by Asian competitors. The 56-year-old Japanese lady has dedicated most of her life to training synchronized swimmers. She has exerted an immeasurable influence on the sport in Asia and even the world. Therefore, she has been honored as the "godmother" in Japan's swimming circles.

As an competitor, she won two gold medals at Japan's National Swimming Championships. When she was 22, Imura took part in the synchronized swimming competition at the Munich Olympics. Unfortunately it was only a demonstration sport then. Imura, who has never won an Olympic gold medal herself, placed her greatest hope on training future swimmers. After graduating from Tenri University, she worked at a middle school in her hometown Osaka as the sports department director. There, she introduced the students to synchronized swimming. At the age of 28, Imura was appointed the head coach for the Japanese national team, and started her glorious coaching life.

Synchronized swimming became an official sport at the 1984 Los Angeles Olympic Games. Miwako Motoyoshi and Saeko Kimura, members of her first team, carried off a bronze medal. Since then, with her attentive instructions, the Japanese team has won medals in all the Olympics. Her team got bronzes in duet and team competitions at the Atlanta, Barcelona and Seoul Olympic Games. And at the Sydney Olympics, Takeda Miho and Tachibana Mira won a silver for her team, the highest Olympic synchronized swimming prize won by Asian athletes. At the 2001 Fukuoka World Aquatic Championships, the same duet won first place, the only championship that had ever been gained by Asians up to then. At the 2004 Athens Olympics, the duet won a silver again, coming next to the Russians, who had been the gold medal holders for years. That made her dejected, and she determined to leave the team. After quitting the coaching job she had held for 26 years, she concentrated on training her swimming club members.

Her success should, in good part, be attributed to her unique understanding of colors and to the unique movements she specially designed to suit her team members. "I decided the colors of all the swimming costumes which should attract the attention of the judges and tell them we are from Oriental Japan," she said. "All other factors should be brought into harmony with our brown eyes, black hair and yellow skin." In the almost three decades of coaching life, Imura choreographed the distinctive Japanese pieces "Ninja", "Sorate", "Wind and Violin", and others for her team. These pieces were well accepted, and helped the Japanese team achieve good results.

If you love them, you rebuke them—the female Hirofumi Daimatsu

In the summer of 2004, Imura published a book titled, "If You Love Them, then Rebuke Them". In the book, she describes in great detail her 30 years of coaching Olympic medal winners and her life as a synchronized swimmer. "If you love them (her charges), you should be strict with them. You rebuke them because you want them to rectify their shortcomings and better their skills," says Imura in the book. "Sharp rebuke is the best way to train them to be the best athletes." These remarks reveal her coaching style, that is, to obtain a remarkable performance as the ultimate goal, and to set strict demands and use sharp rebukes as the means. Combined in training, these two factors are the guarantee of good results.

In Japanese swimming circles, Masayo Imura is called "the female Daimatsu Hirofumi". Hirofumi is famous for his ruthless methods in training his women's volleyball team. A lady with an unyielding personality, Imura coached with feverish ardor. "I will never conceal what I want to speak out. I will never regret and will never give in even if I have to use harsh words or make mistakes," she emphasized. Indeed, we have seen in her a shadow of the volleyball coach Daimatsu Hirofumi training his "Oriental Witches".

When training her club members or coaching the national team, Imura demands that the trainees stay in the water at least eight hours a day, sometimes even 13 hours, plus two hours of off-pool training in coordinating their steps and musical beats. In addition, they have to spare some time watching and studying videos of their training. From the Olympic bronze medalists

Miwako Motoyoshi and Saeko Kimura to the Olympic silver holders Takeda Miho and Tachibana Mira, none of her team members escaped suffering every hell to the point of sniveling under her coaching. "If crying could help you win gold medals, I would do that for you, no matter how long and how hard," Imura would tell the girls when seeing them in tears. Coach Imura is very strict with the team, and there is no such word as "impossible" in her dictionary, Takeda Miho recalled. "We are finished if you say impossible. There is nothing impossible," Imura was quoted as saying. Her severe daily rebukes have established pathways for these Japanese girls from the pool to the Olympic podium.

Devoting her life to synchronized swimming; relaxing most with her dog

Imura was born in 1950, the youngest of the four children of a lumber supplier family in Osaka. Her parents sent her to a swimming club when she was a third grader. She transferred to a new club in her first year at middle school. At the new club, she had more training items and better training conditions. "What a gorgeous sport synchronized swimming is!" her mother once said when Imura was still vacillating in deciding between regular and the synchronized swimming. Mom's unintentional acclamation helped Imura finally make up her mind.

"Actually I wanted to be a painter when I was a kid," Imura said of her childhood dream. "I have pretty good painting skills. A classmate of mine at elementary school participated in an art exhibition with a painting and got a prize for it. But I never told anybody that the painting was my work." Instead of being a painter, she became deeply attached to synchronized swimming. It has been 40 years since she started to engage in the sport, starting from her middle school days. After retiring from the synchronized swimming team, she went back to her old school in Osaka as a temporary employee training young swimmers, with a wage of only 1,000 *yen* a day (equivalent to the average Japanese hourly pay now). Nevertheless, she never wavered in her dedication to synchronized swimming education. Her living conditions remained unchanged until she got married in 1977 to a sports teacher, who was her colleague, and became the coach of Japan's national team the following year. "I am really very happy," Imura said.

Imura, who doesn't have children of her own, has spent most of her time training young swimmers during the past 30 years. She left her coaching post after the Athens Olympic Games to set up a synchronized swimming club of her own, still spending a great amount of time with youngsters. It is the most relaxing time for her when she is with "Satake", her pet dog named after a Japanese anime Ninja figure. Satake, a six-year-old Swiss shepherd streaked with black, white and yellow colors, is a meek and gentle companion. "It is a pity I can't bring him over to China," Imura said.

Dispute with Japan's Synchronized Swimming Committee

At the Doha Asian Games in 2006, the Chinese synchronized swimming team dethroned Japan, the long-time gold medal holder in Asia, in both duet and team events. Soon after came the news that Masayo Imura would head the Chinese team. That caused a great sensation in Japan's news media and in synchronized swimming circles, much of the reaction being disapproving.

But Imura told them, "China is to be the host of the 2008 Olympic Games. Japan's international image in sports will be enhanced and its contribution to synchronized swimming will be prominently displayed if I coach the host's national team. I believe what I have done is correct. Besides, I haven't yet managed to help a team win an Olympic gold medal, and I want to get new coaching experience in China."

She told some Chinese and Japanese reporters, "I am here in China for the betterment of synchronized swimming and for Sino-Japanese friendship. Please don't misunderstand me. You will see that more clearly after 2008. And my particular thanks go to Chinese journalists for their support."

Nowadays, except for the narrow-minded Japanese Synchronized Swimming Committee, Japanese public opinion and the news media are showing more understanding of Imura's position.

Imura in the eyes of Chinese: amicable and dedicated

Ever since Imura took over the Chinese national team she has deeply impressed the team with her unique way of conduct. Amazed at their excellent bodily shapes, Imura lavished the highest praise on the girls. "They are talented girls with slender figures and the most beautiful legs in the world. But unfortunately they lack strength and speed, and their technique of artistic expression leaves much to be desired." So, accordingly, Imura started a course of strict and seemingly "cruel" training to get rid of these weaknesses. The girls practiced almost every day from 8 a.m. till 8 p.m. "I drove them to practice until they said, 'No more, please.' I hope some day they will say they were lucky to have me here with them." The swimmers were a bit afraid

Imura is kind and gentle outside training hours.

of her at first. They had formed close ties with their Chinese instructors after years of going through thick and thin together. But Imura was different. The most agonizing time was strength training, which is Imura's special method. When doing push-ups, for example, she would demand the swimmers do it with an inflatable ball beneath their feet and not bend the back. In flexibility training, she insisted on the swimmers keeping their balance in a correct pose, and wouldn't let them stop until they reached the desired joint range of motion. But the effectiveness of this tough training soon became obvious, and their strength rapidly increased.

"She does everything together with us, except jumping into the pool, setting a good example by practicing what she preaches," Ms. Huang, a team member from Shanghai, said of her Japanese coach. "She is always on the spot, and corrects erroneous movements when we have off-pool practice or body training. She summons us to the side of the pool, and explains to us when she sees anything that doesn't come up to her requirements. You know what the first Chinese words she learned were? 'Ascending', 'Descending', 'Wrong' and 'Stop'. We admire her very much." Jiang Tingting, one of the twin sisters, said, "She is courageous and very stern during training, but very kind and gentle outside training. We all love her very much. We also know her favorite Chinese food is steamed dumplings." Zhang Xiaohuan, a veteran

member of the team from Beijing, said, "We met Imura long ago, at the 2002 Asian Games in Pusan, South Korea. She came over to say hello to us and spoke highly of our performance. It seems we have been brought together by fate. We feel great admiration for her accomplishments. She always emphasizes the standardization of performance both in training and competition. None of us thinks she is cruel; we are all of the opinion that she is very amicable."

Yu Li, an official with China's Swimming Center in charge of water polo and synchronized swimming, said, "Imura, a typical Japanese coach, is highly dedicated to her career. Before the Melbourne world championships she used to work as non-resident coach for our team. Every time she would go to the training center directly from the airport and then directly back to the airport when she finished her training task, working over a dozen hours a day. In fact she is a very kind and charming lady, always wearing a smile. To my knowledge, she is not as ruthlessly stern to the Chinese girls as to the Japanese swimmers. Maybe because she thinks we are foreigners."

Donating to earthquake relief and protecting Beijing's reputation

Coach Imura seldom shows up on public occasions, since she spends most of her time with her team members at the pool. But whenever she gets the chance she tries to do something for Sino-Japanese friendship.

Meeting Japanese reporters after the Olympic qualification competition at the Water Cube, Imura answered a question about the air quality in Beijing: "Please tell Japanese visitors that the air here is very clean and the environment is very beautiful. I have been living here for more than a year,

Imura congratulates her team members after the Chinese team won the Olympic bronze medal in 2008.

and know that some news reports about Beijing's air pollution are not true. Tell people that there is no need to wear masks in Beijing." At a charity event organized by the sports authorities for Sichuan earthquake relief early in 2008, Imura made a generous donation. As a survivor of the 1995 Osaka-Kobe earthquake, she encouraged her team members from Sichuan and said, her eyes brimming with tears, "I know exactly the feelings you have now. I had a similar experience. After the Osaka earthquake, our swimming pool was ruined, and we lost contact with our team members. But we resumed our training only three days after the quake. We had to rent a pool. We had to walk several hours to the pool since all transportation facilities had been destroyed. I will never forget that special moment. You won't be able to go home now, but I hope you will encourage your people with your hard work and great achievements. Now we are preparing ourselves for the Olympics and we should do a better job of heightening their morale."

Beijing Olympic Games: first Olympic medal

Imura made her dream come true when the Chinese team won its first Olympic medal—bronze medal. One day in Beijing's Beihai Park, Imura saw an old man practicing calligraphy on the paved ground with a big sponge writing brush and water. On a whim, Imura took the brush, and wrote the four characters "Hua Yang" and "You Yong" in Chinese, which mean "Synchronized Swimming". The old man said, "I saw you on TV."

In September 2008, Imura bade a reluctant farewell to China. "The stint of one year and eight months here has left me the most blissful memories," she said. She added that she was happy with her deeper understanding of the country. "China and Japan share similarities, and have a long history of exchanges. The two countries can be good neighbors with mutual understanding of each other."

As regards her future plan, Imura said she came to China with the goal of leading the Chinese team to compete at the Olympic Games. But she sincerely hopes that "China and

Writing the words "Synchronized Swimming" with a huge writing brush and water in Beihai Park.

Visiting the Forbidden City, August 31, 2008.

Japan will promote their exchanges to a much higher level, which would have been unimaginable when I first came to China." China is so close to Japan that she will surely visit here again. She said she wondered why Europeans had always won the gold medals at the Olympic Games when watching three national flags hoisted on the Olympic rostrum. "Why shouldn't China and Japan have their national flags flying high there? The two countries should carry out more exchanges, and learn from each other to strive to be the champions of Asia and to be the world champions as well. I believe we will surely achieve this goal!"

By Liu Ailin

Translated by Yang Yaohua

Photos provided by Wang Xiaoyan and www.sportsphoto.cn

Personal File

Name: Christine Cornet

Chinese Name: Ke Rong

Nationality: French

Occupation: Teacher & diplomat

Time in China: 2 years

Her Spring Is in China

She is an expert on China, and her dream is to make more contributions to Chinese culture.

With a deep love for Chinese culture, she has been engaged in Sino-French cultural exchanges and interaction. A trip to China after her graduation from high school ignited her passion to know more about this country, where she found the goal of her lifetime. Since then, this intellectual French lady has enjoyed living and working in China, a pleasure as warm and enchanting as spring.

Short blond hair, a delicate and lean face, and a pair of eyes shining even behind her glasses—that's the first impression Christine Cornet gave me.

That day, as the cultural commissioner at the French Embassy, Christine Cornet presided over a seminar of the works of Ji Dahai, a Chinese painter resident in France. On the occasion, she mentioned that Ji Dahai's painting skills had inherited the style of Ba Da Shan Ren, a master painter at the turn of the Ming and Qing dynasties. I couldn't help wondering, how could a Frenchwoman have such love for and profound understanding of Chinese history and culture?

The spring of cultural exchange has come to China

In the diplomats' apartment building in Sanlitun, I interviewed Christine Cornet. Wearing a necklace with bright-colored beads and a belt knitted with colorful threads, she radiated with a Chinese bearing while her eyes reflected the grace and scholarliness of a French lady.

Freshly returned from Suzhou, she was still enthralled with presiding

over the Huqiu Poetry Session. She told me that the theme of this session was "China—the spring of poets". Several famous contemporary French poets, such as Marcel Relar, Jean-Claude Pinson and Philippe Beck were specially invited to China for communication and poetry exploration with Chinese poets. "A unique aspect of the session was that Chinese poets read French poems in French, and French poets read Chinese poems in Chinese," she said. "It was extremely well received."

"What is the purpose of such poetic communication activities?" Christine Cornet had her own ideas: "In today's pan-materialized world, it seems that poetry has been neglected. Now there are fewer poetry lovers in China than before, and some people even regard poetry as old-fashioned and poets as ancient people. The same is true in France as well." Through poetry communication activities like the Huqiu Poetry Session, Christine strives to restore people's nostalgic feelings for poetry and the poetic spirit, both in China and in France.

"People shall also protect poetry during their pursuit of commercialization, be it ancient or new-born, because it's part of their culture," Christine stressed. Her Chinese is as soft and gentle as her French, but with firm strength.

Shouldering the mission of promoting Sino-French cultural communication and cooperation, Christine has lots of things to do. She elaborated to me on the "Fu Lei Scheme". She said, "Just like the 'Pushkin Scheme' in Russia, the 'Cervantes Scheme' in Spain and the 'Tagore Scheme'in India, the 'Fu Lei Scheme' is a publication-funding plan established by the Ministry of Foreign Affairs of France, which has so far funded the translation and publication of more than 650 French books in China. It's no small feat." She Added, "I'm responsible for the comprehensive qualification examination of publishers, publication projects and translators that have applied for the funds, and will provide funding when appropriate."

In 2005, the French Cultural Center was established in Beijing, opening to the public a multi-media library with a floor area of more than 600 square meters to provide Chinese people with miscellaneous information about French society and culture, and organize communication between French and Chinese publishers. "Apart from that, we also provide professional training for translators, publishers and library administrators, and fund some Chinese retail bookstores so that more French books can be available for Chinese readers."

Christine was happy to see that a growing number of Chinese publishing houses had translated and published books about French culture and society. Meanwhile, more and more Chinese books have been introduced to France. "We are going to hold activities like the 'Readers' Festival' and 'Reading Day', and are now making arrangements for a 'Reading Day' for children and young people (including college students). Moreover, I intend to invite French writers to visit primary schools in Beijing for interactive communication." She told me in high spirits and with a smile.

Remote China opened a window in her heart

Talking about how she came to China and came to love Chinese culture so much, Christine told me in detail.

"It was in 1976, when Zhou Enlai and Mao Zedong passed away, that I became interested in China." She was then 15 years old and still studying at high school. During that time, lots of reports and articles on China were published in newspapers, and one of her teachers especially gave her an introduction to China, which altogether greatly inspired her thirst for knowledge and longing for the remote land of China, a country with a totally different economic system from France. "I wanted to have a thorough understanding of China's history and current situation," she explained. She read all kinds of books about China—almost every book written by French sinologists. She carefully collected these books and took them with her wherever she went.

In 1981, when she graduated from high school, she studied international relations at a renowned policy research institute. Eventually, she got an opportunity to travel to China: "That was a very interesting trip. I took a train through the Soviet Union to Beijing, passing Moscow, Lake Baikal, Harbin, Changchun, Jilin, Shenyang and Dalian before I finally arrived at the capital. This journey offered me some perceptual cognition of China, and on my way home I made up my mind to study Chinese so as to learn more about the country's history and culture."

After studying Chinese history at a university in Paris, Christine came to Fudan University in China to study Chinese. Out of her special interests in Chinese history, she carried out some on-site investigations during her study of the Jiangnan Shipyard, which was established in 1865 with technical cooperation with Britain, and finished her doctoral dissertation titled, *China's Development of Civilization in the 19th and 20th Centuries Reflected through the Jiangnan Shipyard*. In 1996 she became an associate professor in the History Department of the Second University of Lyon in France, where she continued to pursue her research into China's history.

In 2000, Christine switched to research on the relationship between image data and history. Taking up this research has much to do with her experience in Shanghai. When she was there, she was always fond of the grand buildings erected by different countries beside the Huangpu River. They are not of pure French, British or German fashion, nor in Chinese style, but buildings with unique characteristics of cultural elements born from a hybrid of Chinese and foreign culture. All these buildings, together with the foreign concessions where they were set up, enchanted her and brought her endless wonders: Why did those foreigners come to China and what was it like in their time? Such questions stirred her soul even when she was in France. Therefore, she continued her research in the direction of her own thoughts, and published her achievements in her first book in 2001: *1849-1946: Collection of Photos of the French Concession in Shanghai*.

An accidental discovery resurrected Chinese pictures hidden for 70 years

Where the next step of her research should go seemed to have brought Christine to a dead end, as she had gone through almost all the documents about China in local archives in Paris and Nantes.

To try her luck, she went back to the archive of Lyon Missionary Church, a miracle took place: There Christine discovered almost 4,000 photos sleeping quietly in a dust-coated metal cabinet—and she was the one to wake up them and the people in them.

The photographer was a French Jesuit priest named Joseph De, who was sent as a missionary to China in 1932. He brought with him the most advanced photographic equipment of his day, and recorded everything that interested him on the way from Shanghai to Beijing via the Grand Canal. After he returned home, he edited his pictures, and donated them to the Jesuit library.

After her discovery of these legendary old pictures, she found more than 300 pieces of glass sensitive films left by Joseph De in the Library of Lyon, and his travel log written on an exercise book from the historical archives of Society of Jesus in another place. In his diary, Joseph De not only wrote down all his account of the trip but also recorded in details the name of the photography equipment and aperture used to take each picture. It was these detailed data that inspired Christine to find a professional person to work with her in the purpose of reviving these dated memories from an angle of art as well as from that

"A man with a basket for carrying fish", one of the historical pictures from "Families on the River".

of history.

One with the fishing baskets, one of the historical pictures from "Families on the River".

At the very beginning of the Year of Sino-French Cultural Communication, the organizing committees in Lyon, France and Shanghai, China received respectively the project proposal named "Image of China in Joseph De's lens" mailed by Christine and her co-author. The story about the Grand Canal deeply attracted the committees. After nearly two years' preparation, the historical pictures 'Families on the River' on the memory of the canal finally returned for home in Jun. 2005.

These old pictures have made a vivid record of the real life of people living alongside the Grand Canal: fishing baskets, hovels, families on sampans, agricultural appliance, women herding ducks, people living by riverside, stevedores taking a rest, and smiling faces of workers…every picture is telling about a story of life. The sincere smiles on different faces reflect the optimistic living attitude of Chinese people in an era full of poverty, diseases and warfares, expressing the photographer's compliments on "the honor of human".

Facing some fading Chinese culture, she's willing to protect them

Perhaps an endowment from God, in 2006 Christine came back to long-parted China as the Cultural Specialist of the French Embassy, a position can't be more suitable for her.

Christine has found her work extremely meaningful. She has discovered many things that Chinese and French share in common in their thinking and

philosophy. "For example, I love the painting style of Ji Dahai, who paints with the traditional skills inherited from the Chinese master painter Ba Da Shan Ren, yet integrating the special skills in French painting as he now lives in Southern France. As a result, you can enjoy the novel and wonderful painting effects created from the fusion of the brilliant traditional cultures of two different countries, which is so gratifying."

The rapid development of China's economy since 1983 when she left China till today has made Christine very happy. She was extremely pleased to see that China is gradually becoming affluent, yet meanwhile her sensitivity has noticed the other side of the coin. "While pursuing economic development, your own culture should be protected and developed as well. Economic growth shall serve as the propeller of cultural progress. However, in the recent 30 years China has neglected protection over its national culture. I've noticed that the young generations of China have little interest in their national culture while many *hutong* (small

A painting by Ji Dahai, a Chinese painter living in France.

alleys) in Beijing have disappeared. That's really a pity." Meanwhile, Christine has also made objective observations in the differences between different areas in the vast land of China. "Gansu Province is totally incomparable to Zhejiang and Jiangsu Province," remarked she.

This "China hand" always has a pure desire to make more contributions to Chinese culture. "Since I take up the cultural communication work between China and France, I'm always considering how to protect Chinese culture through my own work and efforts. This is of great importance!"

Engaged in Sino-French cultural communication and interaction with a deep love for Chinese culture, the intellectual lady Christine is enjoying her life and work in China, a pleasure as warm and enchanting as spring.

By Zhang Hua
Translated by Yin Jianlei

Personal File

Name: Yury Ilyakhin

Nationality: Russian

Occupation: Businessman

Time in China: 10 years

The Most Chinese-Minded Russian

He is from Russia, and has an inextricable bond of affection for China. He has put in stints as a journalist, an editor, a translator, and, recently, a business owner. He was chosen as a torchbearer for the torch relay in China when the Olympic Games were held in Beijing in 2008. The Russian gentleman, fond of Pu'er tea and Peking Opera, was possessed by his "China dream" over a casual Chinese dinner. That meal completely altered his life's journey.

*Y*ury Ilyakhin, 53, is often said to be the most Chinese-minded Russian, for he has readily adapted to the difference between the two cultures and successfully carved out careers in both lands. He took part in the Olympic torch relay in the city of Lanzhou in July 2008. His indissoluble bond with China has rendered him popular in the news media of the two countries.

Inextricable bond with China

He started forming his attachment to China during the years when Sino-Soviet relations were sour. He enrolled at Moscow State University in 1972, specializing in the Chinese language. The tremendous amount of Chinese characters; the hard-to-learn four tones of the pronunciation; the deteriorated Sino-Soviet relations, all made Yury depressed and confused. However, a casual Chinese gourmet meal changed all that for him.

In the autumn of 1972 he and some schoolmates were invited to a friend's home. His friend's mother is a Chinese working at the Peking Hotel in Moscow, and is good at cooking Chinese food. That day, the mother entertained the group with *Jiaozi*, or boiled dumplings. "No food is more delicious

Yury with his wife at the foot of the Great Wall.

than *Jiaozi*," as the Chinese saying goes. The delectable Chinese food left a deep imprint on his memory. Everybody was sipping Chinese liquor while enjoying the boiled dumplings and fried rice with mushrooms. In the typical Chinese atmosphere of warmth, Yury hit upon an idea: He had to go to China in person, and have a look at how the Chinese people lived.

"Chinese culture is just like a door or a book," he said. "Once you open it, you find it always at your side. You cannot but be affected by the profound cultural heritage of the country's 5,000-year history once you get in touch with it." Maybe because of the charm of Chinese culture, Yury stuck to his Chinese studies to the end.

After graduation, Yury worked as a reporter at the Beijing office of the Russian news agency TASS. Afterwards, he returned to Moscow and worked first at the Asian department of Moscow State Library and then the Russian Publishing House as an editor. During this period, in the 1990s, he translated, edited and published many classical works of Chinese literature, including

Poetry of the Song Dynasty. We have to admit it is a tremendous challenge to express the feelings of ancient Chinese poets in the contemporary Russian language. Reading the graceful and elegant poems of the ancients and experiencing the gamut of their emotions, "I felt very close to these poets," Yury said.

In all his years in China, Yury has cherished affection for Peking Opera, the quintessence of Chinese culture. His favorites are *Farewell, My Concubine* and *Madame White Snake*. He compiled *A Primer of Peking Opera*, a Chinese-Russian bilingual book on *Reading Peking Opera*, *Watching Peking Opera* and *Listening to Peking Opera*. He feels greatly elated when he imagines his fellow-countrymen enjoying the beautiful arias of *Farewell My Concubine* while going through the primer and other stories of Peking Opera he has written. "Cultural exchanges start from literature exchanges," Yury said, "I feel very honored to take part in it."

A scholarly businessman

Yury has been engaged in business in China with great enthusiasm since 1996. He was the founder of "Hand to Hand", a free classified ad medium in Chinese. Now he is the CEO of the Beijing Hand to Hand Information Technology Company. To many Chinese, he is worthy of the title of "scholarly businessman".

Many people doubted that he could make profits from free classified advertisements. But, as he explained, because it's free of charge the information it carries is highly trustworthy; because it's free, there are more clients coming for his business. Abundant and trustworthy information is a sizeable

fortune in itself. With this "give and take" principle in mind, it isn't difficult to understand why Yury's business is thriving.

Most of his employees are Chinese. He was a bit worried at first that it probably wouldn't be easy to lead and team up with the business-oriented Chinese. However, Yury, who is fully acquainted with Chinese culture, knows the old Chinese saying very well: "When in a strange place, follow the local customs," which means "When in Rome, do as the Romans do." Before long he got used to the Chinese mode of thought, and at the same time his employees got to know their foreign boss well, too. They call him "Chief Yury".

In this way, Yury wholeheartedly provides his services to the ordinary Chinese people. He feels proud of his work: "I got a letter from a disabled customer in 2000 who told me that he had found a job for his younger sister through our business. It was the highest praise for our work." He continued, "Every day many newcomers to Beijing who don't have much money try to find jobs or rent accommodation through the information we provide. We are doing our bit for the construction of China's harmonious society." These sincere words from his heart convinced us that he is really very Chinese-minded.

China had been practicing its open-door policy for just five years when Yury came to China. He has witnessed all the changes that have taken place in the country: "Clothes have changed; hair styles have changed; there are more commodities, more hotels, and more restaurants; and poverty has gradually disappeared. But the biggest change of all is that China has opened its door to the whole world. China is having a positive impact on the whole world. Its people respect traditions, and welcome foreigners and their advanced experience, know-how and assistance to come to China. This is an opening of the minds of the Chinese people."

He went on, "In the 1990s I bought a copy of the *Enterprise Law of China*, after I had decided to launch a company here. The book was in both Chinese and English. In the 1980s and 1990s China already had such legal tools to help those who wanted to invest in China." He thinks he is lucky to have learned Chinese and even luckier to have caught up with a flourishing era in China.

The 163 torchbearer

Maybe it was another predestined piece of luck when, in September 2007, Yury came across a piece of news in the *China Daily* that Lenovo, a Chinese PC maker, was looking for eight torchbearers from among foreigners living in China for the Olympic Games, to be selected on the basis of essays they wrote about China. In just one night he wrote "China and I", a short article for the competition, and was chosen as one of the eight.

There was an interesting episode during the voting process. Two hours before the deadline for the vote, Yury was happily watching his ever-increasing account of votes. Suddenly he noticed something was going wrong! His account was instantly and geometrically growing. "There must be someone using an automatic voting method to canvass for me," he thought. "I felt so bad at that time."

The next morning he wrote a letter to Lenovo and its co-sponsor, the *China Daily*. "Participation in the Olympic torch relay represents the Olympic spirit. We should respect ourselves as well as others. I ask the organizing committee to remove the fake votes from my account or delete

me completely from the list of nominees. I would like to be a torchbearer, but have to respect the principles of the Olympics," he said in the letter.

The organizer paid due attention to the issue. After recounting the votes, Yury finished seventh, with 6,751 votes. "Upon hearing the news that I had been elected as one of the torchbearers of the Beijing Olympic Games," he recalled later, "I felt like one of the happiest people in the world."

After that, Yury changed his way of life a little bit. In order to keep in good shape, he reduced the number of beers he drank and started to take a walk every day. "It is a great honor for me to be a torchbearer," he said proudly. "I will do it not only on my own behalf, but also on behalf of the Russian people." Every day he would check the torch relay activities online and collect papers that carried torch relay news. "The Olympic Games have elevated my spirit, and enriched my life. Friends say I am younger now," he said.

It could be imagined how happy his wife and daughter were when they got the news. His wife specially made a big torch-shaped cake, and invited friends for a celebration. Many friends in Russia sent him e-mails asking how he was preparing for the relay and how Beijing was preparing for the Games.

He went to Lanzhou in Northwest China as the 163rd bearer in July 2008. It was his first time to visit the city. He recalled his impression at that time: "With the torch in my hand, I felt I was the happiest man in the world. In my whole life I have never seen so many happy people. May the Beijing Olympic Games be a big success! Let's go all out for it!" Holding the torch high, Yury thought it was "the most unforgettable 50 meters I had traveled in all my life." He waved to the cheering people standing on both sides of the road while running with the torch and shouting together with them: "Go! Go!

Torchbearer 163 races along a street in Lanzhou.

Olympics!"

His wife and daughter, who had come specially from Moscow, joined him all the way to Lanzhou and recorded the unforgettable moment by taking numerous pictures of his relay.

Moskovsky Komsomolets, a leading newspaper in Russia, covered his participation at full length. His elder brother, who works in Moscow, bought 300 copies of the paper, and distributed them among friends and colleagues to share his joy with them.

Conveying friendship through songs

When speaking of Yury, we should not forget to mention his wife Katya. In 2003, Katya founded the Beijing Hand to Hand Choir. The choir members are all Chinese. They rehearse once a week. They sing Russian, Chinese, Italian and German songs. The conductor is Katya, who graduated from the Gorky Academy of Music. Under her diligent instruction, the choir

A perfect couple

has formed its own style: the profound heritage of European classic music combined with the rich Chinese tradition of song. The choir won first place at the Beijing Choir Festival in 2007.

Katya has fostered a keen interest in the *guqin*, a stringed Chinese musical instrument of the zither family. "The *guqin* has a history of almost 2,000 years," she explained. "It looks simple, but there are more that 120 plucking methods for even one single melody on the instrument." The deep understanding of Chinese culture by this musical family would make many native Chinese feel ashamed of their scanty knowledge of their own culture.

Yury loves Uygur folk songs like "When we are young" and "Alamuhan", as well as Chinese folk songs like "Sea! My hometown" and "Jasmine". He stressed, "Music brings about a better mutual understanding among people. The beautiful Chinese songs are so moving that they bring tears to my eyes. The same is true of the tuneful Russian songs that are so touching that they make the Chinese choir members tingle with excitement. China and

Getting together in China.

Russia are big neighbors, and both have profound cultural heritages. We have a harmonious atmosphere in the Hand to Hand Choir."

It's not easy to reach an understanding between countries, people say. But Yury's experience has proved how simple it can be.

The Hand to Hand Choir gave an Olympic-themed concert in Beijing in August, and the whole family thoroughly enjoyed the Olympic gala in their adopted homeland.

By Li Tao

Translated by Yang Yaohua

Personal File

Name: Leonardo Posada

Chinese Name: Lai Ao

Nationality: Colombian

Occupation: Businessman

Time in China: 25 years

Don't Take Me As a Foreigner

Though a 100% foreigner, he has 100% Chinese feelings. Born in Colombia, he grew up in China. As a revolutionary descendant, he didn't succeed to his fathers' cause. Nevertheless, he is supporting Chinese socialist construction and making contributions to Chinese and the world's economic progress in another way. He has many unusual stories about China. He went through thick and thin during that passionate period and witnessed the tremendous changes brought about by reform. Let us get close to Leonardo, a foreigner who regards himself as Chinese.

*L*eonardo Posada is Colombian, though not so occidental as most Westerners. His slightly high nose and somewhat curling hair make him resemble the minority people in Xinjiang, China. Before I estimated his height, he blurted out, "One six eight, meaning well-heeled". His idiomatic Beijing accent makes him even less like a foreigner.

He grew up and was educated in China. He has numerous classmates, friends and relatives in China. They call him Lai Ao, or Liuer. In his 48 years, he has spent about more than half of his time in China. Few foreigners have gone deeper into or stayed longer in Chinese society than he has. After moving around on the other side of the world, he finally returned to China. His friends never take him as a foreigner despite his role as a representative of an American investment company, for he has already become part of China's flesh and blood.

Those unforgettable days in the heat of the sun

Since the founding of the PRC in 1949, the Friendship Hotel in northwestern Beijing has been receiving foreign experts assisting China and

their families. It is here that Lai Ao grew from a child into a young man. He showed us around the hotel.

He pointed out to us the building where he once lived, the swimming pool (now a gym) and the shop. Now, however, everything has changed, and Lai Ao could no longer find any acquaintances there.

Leonardo first came to China in 1964 at the age of four.

Influenced by Maoism, his father Enrique Posada came to China, and made great contributions to China's Spanish-language teaching and translation of important documents. He translated and was responsible for the finalization of the Spanish version of the *Selected Works of Mao Zedong*, thus winning a long-standing reputation in Chinese translation circles. After that, the Spanish versions of both the *Selected Works of Chen Yun* and the *Selected Works of Deng Xiaoping* came out thanks to his authoritative collation.

Enrique Posada was a respected old friend of the Chinese people, and he had enjoyed first-class courteous treatment in China. Chinese leaders of the older generation, including Mao Zedong and Deng Xiaoping, received him and other foreign experts who assisted China's construction many times, and Leonardo took advantage of that. "I saw Premier Zhou many times, too many times to remember, but now I can't find the picture of him holding me in his arms." The Chinese people bear deep respect for these international friends with whom they went through thick and thin. Deng Xiaoping, Jiang Zemin and Hu Jintao expressed their thanks many times to these foreign experts, who have made outstanding contributions to the Chinese people.

Leonardo's parents worked at the University of International Relations

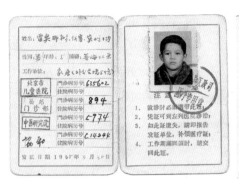

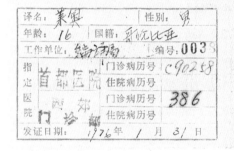

Leonardo's old medical care card and student card.

when they first arrived in China. Later, his father was transferred to the Central Compilation and Translation Bureau. In kindergarten Leonardo was favored by the teachers not for his father's position but for his smart and lovely look. He spoke Spanish at home and Chinese at the kindergarten, which was the beginning of his bilingual education.

Then he went to study at the Red Temple Primary School in Fenzi Lane, Xicheng District. The school was near his father's workplace, so his father could take him to school and back. That was why his parents chose that school.

Lai Ao's full name Leonardo Posada was hard for his classmates

and teachers to pronounce. For convenience his mother asked one of her co-workers, Aunt Yang, to give Leonardo a Chinese name, and this name was supposed to be connected with his seven-year-old brother's. "My brother was physically weak, and mom hoped he could get strong, so he was called Li Songqiang (meaning healthy). Mom hoped my name could sound and sunny, so I was named Li Xiangyang (meaning always facing the sun)." This name came from an anti-Japanese hero in the movie Guerrillas on the Plains, and few Chinese don't know it. "Aunt Yang didn't take that movie into account. The name was actually derived from my brother's," he said. But Leonardo is not clear why Li was chosen as his family name. Perhaps it was because Li is the most common family name in China.

Leonardo returned to Colombia together with his parents in 1970, and came back to China to study in 1972.

He spent several years at Yuying Junior High School, and then another few years at Beijing No.172 Senior High School, which afterwards became the High School Affiliated to Renmin University of China. Many students of both schools came from the families of cadres, military officers and foreign experts, and all of them liked hanging around with Leonardo. During the "cultural revolution", adults were engaged in revolutionary movements, so the children were out of control and ran amok. "At that time I committed every bad deed a boy could, like fighting, being absent from school and grabbing girls." said Leonardo. Many years after that, when Leonardo saw the movie *In the Heat of the Sun* he felt that the movie was a mirror of his childhood.

During his high school days few people called him Li Xiangyang. They called him Lie Ou, Lai Ou or other names phonetically similar to Lai Ao.

Once some cunning guy pronounced his name Lai Ao into one word sounding like Liuer (phonetically "six" in Chinese). It was easy to pronounce, and thus became very popular. Without knowledge of Leonardo's family one might think he was the sixth child of his parents and had five older brothers and sisters.

In many occidental languages Leo means lion. It seems parents all over the world hope their children will grow up to be strong and promising. But teachers and parents could by no means figure out how Leo became Liuer. Anyway, everything was all right as long as Leonardo accepted it.

Even today he can tell who is speaking on the other end of the phone judging from the way the caller addresses him—as "Li Xiangyang", "Lie Ao" or "Liuer"—and then he knows that he is an acquaintance from primary school, high school or college.

High school is an amorous period of time. It was in high school that Leonardo began to have ideas about beautiful girls. The so-called dating girls now was called grabbing girls in those days. The different wording shows the distinct characteristics of different times. You can't grab a girl now; instead, you must be soft, careful and romantic. But in those days girls were extremely straightforward and tough, and they despised romantic stuff. Romantic was not a good word then, and to be romantic deserved punishment.

Finally Leonardo was about to grab a girl. One of his friends gave him a chance to be with his ideal girl alone. The place for the appointment was chosen as Purple Bamboo Park. The two children had a nice talk, and it seemed very hopeful. Later, however, the romance came to a halt for the girl kept evading him. He had no idea why, and then his first love failed for

no reason. Thirty years later, his teacher (a headmaster today) told him the secret: "Our school treasured you guys from foreign families, and watched you closely in case of any accident. When we found you two were in love we could only warn the Chinese girl to keep away from you." The teachers stopped their love for a good purpose.

Leonardo still meets that girl at alumni parties. Their calf love is past, yet it hasn't vanished like fog. He just keeps this beautiful memory in his mind forever.

The early bird didn't catch the early worm

Leonardo went to school very young and just in time. When he graduated from senior high school, the college entrance exam came back after being suspended for ten years. Leonardo grabbed this chance, entered Beijing Medical College (now the Beijing University Health Science Center) and majored in clinical medicine. This was specially approved by Geng Biao, former minister of the Foreign Liaison Ministry. Trouble came when he was a junior. His parents had returned to Colombia, and his residence became a problem. Colombia hadn't established diplomatic relations with China, so he couldn't get a new passport or visa. Thus he was forced to go back to Colombia in 1981.

For the same reason, China and Colombia didn't recognize each other's educational diplomas. A medical diploma and medical qualifications didn't count unless in the countries and areas of the same language. Leonardo had to face the differences between Chinese and Colombian high school curriculums, and tried to pass the Colombian exams using the knowledge he had acquired in China. In the end, Leonardo switched his major to economics and finance. This postponed his graduation until 1988. "The early bird didn't catch the early worm," sighed Leonardo.

After graduation, Leonardo entered financial circles in Colombia, and worked hard for the European Community's loan programs for low-income groups. In 1993, Leonardo led a Colombian trade delegation to China, and was back in Beijing again after ten years . The great changes that had taken place in the course of China's reform and opening up impressed Leonardo, and made him determined to live here once again.

In 1998 he began to work in the Beijing office of Santander Central Hispano S.A., where he stayed for eight years. In the meantime, Leonardo changed his Chinese name to Bo Sada. His next move was to join a US investment company, as he thought that his work at the bank lacked challenge and adventure.

In the movie *A World Without Thieves* the hero says, "What's the most valuable thing in the 21st century? Talent." This has become a popular saying in China in recent years. But only Americans really know the importance of talent and are good at digging out and making good use of it. Leonardo received both a Chinese and a Colombian education, worked in the Hispanic finance industry and made his reputation in China. People like him tend to fall prey to Chinese headhunters.

His new position was that of business development representative. His information processing skills and ability to judge investment projects and solve problems due to his good connections in China brought him high trust and a good salary from this American investment bank.

Leonardo has a good harvest both in career and love. Seeing him driving

his beautiful wife and adorable daughter to parties, all new and old friends can feel the heat the happy family gives off.

The early bird didn't catch the early worm, but he caught a big one, big enough to make him titter.

Knitting happy days

"All the days come here, let me knit you," intoned a poet. This seems to be a depiction of Leonardo's mood after he returned to China. After he met Wang Yan, he knitted every single day of his life into a happy one.

Seeing him living alone, his classmates and friends in Beijing began to make chances for him to date girls. Finally at a party, when he met elegant and beautiful Wang Yan, he felt she was his ideal woman, and immediately he began his love campaign. "May I go to your house for a cup of coffee?" "Maybe the other day." Wang Yan flushed. Leonardo saw hope, so he continued, asking to go to her house for a coffee the same day. As a CCTV playwright-director, Wang Yan is a modern woman, yet she couldn't withstand his fierce attack.

What was the result? Leonardo smiled like a successful conspirator. "I drank everything in her house except coffee." All his friends laughed. His eager entreaty forced Wang Yan to let him go to her house, but she didn't serve him coffee, which was a deliberate cold shoulder. But whether he drank coffee or not didn't matter at all, for Leonardo had found a person with whom he could knit a happy life in the future.

Their first nest was in the Beijing Youth Apartment Building. The small flats in the building are designed for new couples. As China

Leonardo with his daughter Manuela.

changed, their nest was constantly upgraded. First they lived in a two-room flat which CCTV allocated to Wang Yan, and then they bought other houses. Now they are living in a big flat measuring over 200 sq m near the Capital Airport. We call this an early step into the well-off standard. "Yeah, well-off." He smiles. In fact they are more than that. After all, as an investment expert he has good investment acumen, so several of their houses are appreciating. Given his current wealth, he can be included in the middle class.

Leonardo and Wang Yan's child was born in the 21st century. This doll-like child has long eyelashes. Her Spanish name is Manuela, and her Chinese

name is Wang Longge. The family name Wang shows Leonardo's respect for his wife, Long (dragon) is the symbol of China, and Ge is phonetically similar to the first syllable of the word Colombia. This name embodies not only Wang's literary talent but also Leonardo's deep feelings for his homeland Colombia and his second homeland China.

Little Manuela is about to begin her school life. Leonardo wants her to go abroad for study, for he is against the fierce competition in the Chinese exam-oriented educational system. "Life is hard for Chinese children. They are almost choked by the curriculum and homework, and hardly have time to play. Education is not supposed to kill children's character. They should play and study rather than be manipulated by grading." Wang Yan experienced the exam-oriented system, and was accepted by a key university. Does she completely agree with Leonardo? We have no idea, but it is said that she is a little worried that Leonardo may spoil their child.

Watching bud-like Manuela, 48-year Leonardo is filled with happiness. How can he not spoil her?

Whatever education she receives, she is definitely going to command several languages. The little girl knows not only her mother's mother tongue and her father's language, but also knows a little English. A promising translator is growing up. But her father is long-sighted: "She should learn a subject first of all, for foreign languages are only tools. What the Spaniards and Americans are interested in is my professional ability, not my languages."

Whether Manuela is going to study in China or abroad will be a topic for Leonardo and Wang Yan for a long time to come.

Once asked if he was a hen-pecked man, Leonardo answered, in a forced masculine tone: "Of course not! In my family I am in charge of big events,

and she is in charge of minor ones. But no big event has happened so far."
We all laughed. Who knows whether where their daughter will be studying is
a big event or not?

Rescuing red and green history

Leonardo and Wang Yan have their own careers, but in recent years they
have found a career that requires their cooperation.

The old experts that took the side of the Chinese revolution in years
gone by, including Leonardo's father, are elderly, and some have passed away
already. Leonardo has visited many of them, and contacts their children from
time to time. Every time he receives an obituary of an old expert Leonardo
and his father lament sadly.

They witnessed the passionate period of China, when the Chinese people
struggled to break blockades for national independence. They took part in
that period with zeal, and paid a high price for it without complaint. Some
of them are enjoying their old age, some of them are leading an unsatisfying
existence, some of them are haunted by illness, some of them are suffering
from miserable conditions, and others, like Leonardo's father, must continue
to work, for their working years in China don't count toward a pension in
their own country. These people are scattered in every corner of the world,
and as time goes by they will inevitably vanish. When they leave, they will
take away some historical memories, which will be a loss to history and to
China.

Deeply worried about this, Leonardo thinks rescuing history is an urgent
task. As a playwright-director of CCTV, Wang Yan understands Leonardo's

idea, and is willing to give him technical support. Their cooperation is going to bring about a result beyond prediction, which makes Leonardo more satisfied with his close pursuit of Wang Yan. "See? Our marriage has been a good deal for me."

To video-record the lives and words of the experts of the older generation is to rescue the Red history that their children have witnessed too. Interestingly, among their children many have returned to China due to their love for China since their childhood. They speak standard Chinese and melt into Chinese society very quickly. They understand the Chinese reform and opening-up policy more quickly and go deeper into the Chinese economic tide than their fathers did. They respect their fathers' commitment, passion and experiences during the Chinese revolution, but they don't repeat their fathers' life course. In the new era, they are turning a new page of Chinese history, writing a new history of the development of the economy of China and the world, and beginning a new period of recording economic costs and achievements with RMB, US dollars or euros. The younger generation is participating in a new history, and Leonardo calls this Green history, reflecting the green color of paper money.

The older and younger generations are both history makers, and Red and Green have both made contributions to China's construction. Red history needs rescuing, and the modern Green history will become past history very soon, and fade away if not recorded. Three generations from now, who will remember the stories of the foreigners of two generations at the beginning of the founding of the PRC and during the reform and opening-up period? We can't wait for Manuela, i.e. Wang Longge, to rescue the history of her father or even her grandfather.

What Leonardo and Wang Yan are doing should be taken as meaningful and altruistic. Good luck to them!

By Lu Yang
Translated by Zhang Ruiqing

Personal File

Name: Yuta Ishiyama

Nationality: Japanese

Occupation: Actor

Time in China: 15 years

Japanese Monkey King on a Chinese Stage

He is not very tall, but he looks fine and delicate, like someone from the south of the Yangtze River. From conversations, you will find that he has a shrewd eye, betraying a bit of smartness. If you do not inquire about his identity, you will never know that he is a foreigner. He is China's first foreign professional Peking Opera actor, the Monkey King from Japan—Yuta Ishiyama.

*O*n stage, he performs tough Peking Opera movements like *Jumping over the Threshold*, winning bursts of applause from the audience. This actor with excellent skills is actually Japanese. He is not only expert at performance, but is also able to chat with everybody using Beijing dialect. His name is Ishiyama Yuta, and he is from Tokyo, Japan.

A predestined relationship with Peking Opera

Yuta was born into a family of office clerks in Tokyo. The 32-year-old Ishiyama, who has lived in Beijing for fifteen years, is an actor with the China National Peking Opera Company. He was awarded by the Ministry of Culture the title of "first foreign professional actor". When I met him he was wearing a Tai-chi amulet on his chest. He is a vegetarian and very familiar with Beijing. There is no shortage of foreigners who study Peking Opera in Beijing, but he is the only one that has followed the profession of a Peking Opera actor.

Yuta has been lively and active since a young age. Not long after he began going to primary school, one day, he turned on the TV, and was deeply

attracted by a monkey played by a man. Later, he learnt that the monkey was called "Qitiandasheng Monkey King", who was good and honest, and especially loved to defend others against injustice. From then on, he became obsessed with Peking Opera, and his obsession finally reached a state where he "not only liked it, but could not do without it."

Journey to the West and *Romance of the Three Kingdoms* are two of China's classical masterpieces which are also very popular in Japan. Sometimes cartoons derived from them are broadcast on Japanese television.

Peking Opera is, after all, China's "national essence". If one does not go to China, and does not learn Chinese, how can one appreciate the charm of Peking Opera? Yuta was determined to go to China to learn Peking Opera, and started looking for an opportunity to learn Chinese. There was a society composed of Japanese Peking Opera lovers in Tokyo—the "Research Institute of Peking Opera". Every weekend, a teacher would be invited to give guidance in training. Yuta joined the children's class of the institute. In his leisure time, he worked hard at learning Chinese. He was the youngest student in his class. From primary to high school, he studied Chinese, and at the same time, he worked hard at the basic skills of Peking Opera.

In 1992, about to graduate from high school, Ishiyama participated in a Chinese speech competition held by Japan's Asahi Shimbun newspaper. He won the first prize with a speech about Peking Opera—a free trip to China in 1993.

In the autumn of 1993, 17-year-old Yuta, alone, set foot in China. Natually, the main purpose of his trip was to watch and learn Peking Opera. He applied to the affiliated middle school of the National Academy of Chinese Theatre Arts in Beijing, and was assigned to affiliated middle school of the Chinese Opera Institute, after an examination. The teachers there thought that he would best perform the roles of greenwood heroes.

Tough training

After coming to China, Yuta found that learning Peking Opera was not an easy task.

In such films as *Farewell My Concubine*, we can see the harshness of the training of actors in the past, in the so-called "big prison for seven years". Now, although masters are no longer so severe with their apprentices, if one wants to achieve success, one cannot slacken off at all. Yuta wanted to be an excellent Peking Opera actor even in his dreams. He knew that in China, in order to achieve their dreams, many people start to practice acting from a very young age, whereas he only started his performance training at the age of 17 when his body was more or less mature. So he had to pay a higher price than others did.

Yuta got up at five o'clock every morning, and went to a nearby park to train his voice and practice reciting lines. In addition, he had to practice such feats as kicking, bending, diving and standing on his head. At first, he could not stand on his head for even two minutes, and later, the teacher tied his ankles to a pole to train him.

Skillful makeup

In addition, his roles called for him to practice

squatting for up to 45 minutes at a time.

There is a saying in Peking Opera circles: "Line reciting weighs one thousand *jin*, while line singing weighs four Liang (measurement of weight, one sixteenth of a *jin*), indicating that in Peking Opera, "line reciting" is more difficult to learn than singing. Different from speaking, each word of "line reciting" has its own rhythm. It is not easy for Chinese people to recite opera lines clearly, let alone Japanese.

Yuta would record the lines recited by his teacher, and repeat them word by word following the tape recorder after school.

Looking back on those days, Yuta said, "I was completely devoted to Peking Opera both physically and mentally, almost forgetting the outside world."

The opportunity finally came

After finishing the four-year course at the school, Yuta passed the entrance exam to the department of performance of the Chinese Opera Institute in 1997. At the institute there was more theory than practice, so after his lessons during the day, Yuta would go to a gym to practice for an extra two or three hours in the evening.

In the summer of 2001, Yuta finally got a college diploma. On the eve of graduation, Japan's NHK television station sent reporters to China to record and report the process of his graduation performance. After the program was broadcast in Japan, many Japanese Peking Opera fans wrote letters of encouragement to him.

On the eve of his graduation at the end of 2000, the news came that the

China National Peking Opera Company was to recruit actors of Yuta's speciality. Yuta took a test, and was accepted.

This was the first appointment of a foreigner as a professional actor in China. However, Wu Jiang, president of the China National Peking Opera Company, was forward-looking, and thought that the art needed a wider range of talent.

In August 2002, Yuta appeared in one of the 17 operas the troupe presented at the Grand Theatre in Beijing—*The Fork in the Road*, in which he played the role of the innkeeper Liu Lihua.

However, during the first of his two performances of this role he was upset by two mistakes he made: Instead of leaping silently onto a table, he slipped and landed on it with a crash, and at one point he dropped his sword. At the following performance, he made sure that he did not repeat these mistakes, and acted flawlessly.

As an example of his professionalism, Yuta showed his versatility when he acted the part of the Monkey King stealing the peaches of immortality. The role required that he jump onto a table where the peaches were, and eat them. However, his landing on the table caused the peaches to roll off it. Quick as a flash, he simply turned a somersault and picked the peaches up, just as a monkey would, and won a special round of applause from the audience.

At the 2003 CCTV Spring Festival Opera Show Yuta got the opportunity to perform with leading clown actors in the opera *Matching with Clowns*, thereby widening his experience with other roles. So far, Yuta has learned parts for over 20 operas, including *Turning the Heavenly Palace Upside Down*, *The Fork in the Road* and *Shiqian Exploring the Way*.

In order to augment his stage experience, Yuta often gave performances,

The peach-stealing scene from *Turning the Heavenly Palace Upside Down*.

especially as the Monkey King, at teahouses in the evening.

Today, Peking Opera is undergoing a revival, and lighting, costumes and stage settings are becoming more and more gorgeous. However, in Yuta's opinion, the marrow of Peking Opera cannot change.

Some people remain puzzled about Yuta, who sacrificed so much to come to Beijing to take up opera. Only those who know him well know that the art of Peking Opera was the goal he had set his mind on. "He is much more hardworking than ordinary students" was his teacher's comment.

Falling in love with the Monkey King role

Yuta has been playing the part of the Monkey King for so many years that he has a unique understanding of the role. He has immersed himself in all the materials he can find about the *Journey to the West*, such as the cartoon movie *Turning the Heavenly Palace Upside Down*, the TV adaptation of the novel, and so forth. His favorite is the movie featuring Steven Chow, a famous Hong Kong comedian.

In order to act the part of the Monkey King with conviction, Yuta often went to the Beijing Zoo to observe the monkeys there closely.

On the 30th anniversary of the normalization of diplomatic relations between China and Japan, Shanghai hosted an exchange of their respective traditional arts by young people from China and Japan. Yan Qin'gu, a Chinese, performed in Ravings (from a traditional type of Japanese opera), while Yuta put on a show of Peking Opera roles.

In September 2008, Yuta and his theatrical troupe performed in Tokyo, which soon became headline news among Peking Opera organizations there. After the performance, he went to middle and high schools to publicize

traditional Peking Opera. He explained the imagery in Peking Opera: a whip representing a horse, an oar representing a boat, the lifting of a foot representing the crossing of a threshold, the movement of both hands representing the moving of a flowerpot, and so forth. Yuta felt

Monkey King is Yuta's favorite role.

The road is long.

that it was not sufficient simply to appreciate the exciting movements and songs in Peking Opera; a deeper understanding of its imagery is necessary. However, he said, "It is difficult to cultivate audiences for Peking Opera because there are too many entertainment alternatives nowadays." Nevertheless, in Yuta's eyes, "the stage is much more fun than movies and TV" and "much more exciting".

Although it takes a skilled actor less than ten minutes to complete his facial makeup, it takes Yuta half an hour, but he insists on doing the job in person. He learns attentively and diligently from the senior actors.

Before he puts on an important show, Yuta invites Liu Xizhong (who was Yuta's teacher in college, a former actor with the National Peking Opera Grand Theatre and a "national first-class actor") to the rehearsal, and asks him for advice. Yuta said that many artists are at the same time gourmets, like Ma Lianliang, who opened a restaurant of his own. From excellent senior actors, Yuta not only learns acting skills, but also a sense of devotion and a rigorous attitude to operatic art.

Apart from the regular physical and vocal exercises, Yuta trains his eyes to assume special expressions that can be communicated to the audience. He

Yuta always does his own makeup.

does this by staring at a lighted incense stick in a dark room, and waving it from side to side. In his opinion, the expression in the eyes is the most difficult to grasp in opera training, for it is something like a sense, and not a physical part of the body.

When being asked about whether all the training and practicing of opera did any harm to his health, Yuta replied in a Beijing accent that he "had troubles everywhere". Indeed, as an acrobatic comedian, injury is hard to avoid.

Living in China for many years, Yuta is quite familiar with the characteristics of different opera fans in different places. There is a saying: "Learn opera in Beijing, win fame in Shanghai and get judged in Tianjin." This reflects the high level of appreciation of Peking Opera fans in Tianjin. Yuta has won praise from the strict Tianjin fans, in addition to the devotion of his fans in Beijing.

By Zhang Hong
Translated by Zhou Gang

Personal File

Name: Kim Chang Back

Nationality: Korean

Occupation: Hockey Coach

Time in China: 9 years

"Teacher" Respected by 1.3 Billion Chinese

In the court, he is a devil. Out of the court, he is like a kind father. At home, he is a dutiful son. In China, he is a patriot. He has a side of an unyielding man and another side of a gentle hero. The Chinese have long thought of him as one of themselves, and he also considers China a bosom friend. He is the foreign head coach of the Chinese national female hockey team, Kim Chang Back.

*A*t the 2008 Beijing Olympics, the Chinese female hockey team led by the Korean head coach Kim Chang Back made history. On August 20, rising from the "death group", the Chinese team defeated the defending champion Germany 3:2, and roared into the final of Olympic women's hockey. Girls of the Chinese team said, "We've made history for China and we are going to make history for the world." In the past, apart from the two silver medals won by the Korean female hockey team led by Kim Chang Back, no Asian teams could shake the leading position of the Westerners in hockey.

But now the Chinese girls, led by their adored "Teacher Kim", are to fight for the gold medal.

Chinese female hockey team makes history

At 8:30 Beijing time, August 22, 2008, the Chinese female hockey team led by Kim Chang Back started to fight for their dream. The short, thin-headed coach with a dark face stood at the edge of the court, watching his students going to the match.

It was in the year 2000, at the Sidney Olympics, that the unknown

Chinese female hockey team won fifth place, which surprised many strong teams: "How could this valiant team appear all of a sudden?" Ever since then, the Chinese female hockey team has grown stronger and stronger. It was under the direction of this iron chief commander, Kim Chang Back from Korea, that the Chinese female hockey team could emerge in such a short time as such a strong team. In 2002, at the World Grand Champions Cup, the Chinese team defeated the world's five top teams and won the world championship. It was the second world championship that China had won in the ball games, the first being by the Chinese female volleyball team.

Four years ago, at the Athens Olympics, the Chinese female hockey team fought to the semi-final, but suffered a loss to Germany on penalty shootouts, and didn't win a medal. Then the strength of Chinese female hockey team declined. After some time at a low ebb, Kim Chang Back inspired the hopes of the Chinese female hockey team again. In fact, at this Olympics, the Chinese team drew the worst lot, and was assigned to a "death group". No one except a few thought they could enter the semi-final. To everyone's astonishment, they made a clean sweep of the other teams. With 3 wins, 1 draw and 1 loss. Losing to the Netherlands and drawing 2:2 with the strong Australian team (thus eliminating it), the Chinese female hockey team entered the semi-final, where twice they fell behind but twice managed to equalize the score, and finally reversed the situation and defeated Germany, taking revenge for the previous Olympics at which they had been defeated by Germany through a penalty.

The girls played for all they were worth. Many times they fell and scraped their skin, but they were never afraid, but just got up and went on fighting. Compared with four years previously in Athens, this team was more

Kim Chang Back explains tactics to his players.

mature, and they deserved a good result more than ever. The Chinese female hockey team—It's been nine years! They've shown us their unyielding spirit and they've sacrificed so much! We believe the moment they entered the court, every one of them must be filled with passion, since it was the final game, and finally they could fight for the championship! For this moment, they had been struggling for nine years under the direction of Kim Chang Back. The team leader Ma Yibo would never forget this day, because she had a tooth knocked out by an opponent's hockey stick. They'd strain every nerve! Just for this dream! It would be the most unforgettable 70 minutes in their lives.

The Netherlands well deserves their top world ranking. They got a chance of a short corner at the very beginning. Then they made one shot after another, but Zhang Yimeng, the goalkeeper of the Chinese team, stopped the ball every time. The Netherlanders made wild attacks and exerted great pressure on the Chinese goalkeeper. After the Netherlands' wild attacks, the Chinese started their counterattack with great patience. The Netherlanders

were active in stealing the ball in midfield so that the Chinese got no chance to break through. Only 13 minutes later could the Chinese make a shot. At 11 minutes from the end of the first half, the Netherlands got a most threatening short corner and made a shot, but Zhang Yimeng stopped the ball. The Netherlands team showed their great overall strength and fine techniques. The Chinese organized many attacks from the right side, and the Netherlands also chose their left side as the major point of attack. It was just diamond cutting diamond. 0:0! The first half ended in a draw.

In the second half, the Netherlands continued to launch a vigorous offensive. Seeing no breakthrough, both teams started to change players frequently to change the tempo, and the game came to a deadlock. The Chinese mainly defended and counterattacked. In the 15th minute of the second half, a Netherlands player scored with a follow shot. Netherlands gained a 1: 0 lead! When there was only eight minutes before the end of the game, No. 11 of the Netherlands scored a goal, thus the Netherlands held a 2: 0 lead. Now the Chinese could no longer reverse the situation. They were consuming too much of their physical strength, but they were still struggling. The Hockey Stadium resounded with a deafening "Go! China!"

The game ended with the Netherlands gaining the gold medal in female hockey in the Beijing Olympics. In excitement, the girls of the Netherlands hugged each other, tears running down their cheeks. The Netherlands had good reason to feel proud, to be sure. However, the Chinese should also get praise though they were defeated, for they had fought heroically to the last minute, against the Netherlands, a team stronger than themselves. And they gained for the Chinese the best result in the team ball games at the Beijing Olympics, better than that of the female volleyball team (bronze medal)

Kim Chang Back smiles after the match.

on which the Chinese had laid great hopes, and that of the female basket-ball team (fourth place) which had been in good form. All the Chinese fans cheered for them, for with a silver medal they had already made history.

But the girls were disappointed. Li Hongxia, a player, said that since they had participated in the game, got a chance to fight for the championship and played for all they were worth, it was really regrettable to have to settle for second place.

A former team leader, now a "super substitute player", Cheng Hui, said it was her third time to play in the Olympics. She had given birth, and then returned to the court. She felt regretful at the result, but she was grateful to Kim Chang Back for giving the Chinese female hockey team this chance.

Kim Chang Back, the head coach, said, "I'm really grateful to the Chinese people and the fans. It is they who give us the power to be here. We

feel regretful for having no gold medal to repay your support. But our players have done their best. I hope the Chinese people can understand. I wished to put gold medals on the girls' necks, and it's a pity we didn't make it. It's really a pity."

Kim Chang Back said he felt lucky to be the coach of the best team in the world, the Chinese female hockey team. "This is the only team I have met in my life as a coach to which I could totally devote myself. I'm afraid that I could never in my lifetime, have such a united team in which everyone thinks of the others as family." He also said, "I'm hot-tempered, and sometimes I was fretful and irritable under great pressure, and they were wronged many times. But in my heart I really love them. They are careful and prudent, have high morale and win people's respect with their perseverance."

At the news briefing after the game, Kim Chang Back showed up with a smile. However, this was just a polite smile, for he said he "was weeping in his heart", for he thought a silver medal could not repay the sweat of the girls of the female hockey team.

"Since I'm facing our journalist friends, and what's more my players exerted their utmost, I have to keep a smile on my face," said this Korean who had worked as the head coach of the Chinese team for nine years, "but I'm weeping in my heart, for the girls have paid too much during the training all these years, sacrificed their peak years. Without a gold medal to repay them, I feel really sorry."

Talking of the sacrifice of the players, Kim Chang Back expressed deep regret. "Look at the Netherlands, how strong and tall they are! Our players are much weaker physically. So if their training lasts two hours, we have to train four hours. On the court, when they need to run two steps, we have to run four. Our players have to train many times harder than the European players to reach or even approach their level."

Kim Chang Back emphasized repeatedly that the Chinese players had played their best. "The Netherlands players are excellent in their techniques and tactics. It's very difficult to defeat them. They are the best players in the world, but ours are also excellent."

Five times participating in the Olympics (twice as the head coach of the Korean hockey team and three times as head coach of the Chinese team) with his teams, Kim Chang Back never gained the highest honor. "An Olympic gold medal is always my dream. But till now I have nothing to regret." The tenacity of Kim Chang Back moved everyone. When China's media considered this historical moment of the Chinese female hockey team as an unimaginable great success, Kim Chang Back said, "To me, it is not a success unless we win the gold medal."

In fact, when we see hockey courts everywhere in the country of tulips and count their millions of hockey players, we would feel it was a glorious defeat since we could challenge them with only a few hockey courts and 2,000 players. The 1.3 billion Chinese are satisfied with the achievement of the female hockey team, and thank Kim—"the devil coach"—wholeheartedly.

The result of an Internet survey shows Kim Chang Back has won the greatest popularity among the foreign coaches China hires. Ninety percent of the netizens hope he can remain as head coach after the Olympics. It seems no one shows disrespect to this coach who won glory for China.

Kim Chang Back doesn't like to be called "Hiddink"

"If we still couldn't win, it must have been be God's will." After they beat Germany 3:2 in the semi-final and roared into the final, Kim Chang Back felt the heavy burden on his heart in the previous four years finally disappeared. His nine years life in China makes him feel he is already one of the Chinese. He hopes to bring an Olympic gold medal for the Chinese female hockey team before he retires. He knows this team needs a gold medal to boost its morale. "Heaven has eyes! They will surely be fairly paid back."

Very few are like Kim Chang Back who set their goal to be the gold medal before every Olympics. But to him, a coach who can't lead his team to victory has no meaning. "It's my career. I must strive to reach this goal. I can't decide who wins, but I'm taking pains all the time to win. I've tried, and therefore I will never regret it. "

As early as in 1988, Kim Chang Back led the Korean female hockey team to the silver medal in the Seoul Olympics. Twenty years later, as the head coach of the Chinese team, he gained another silver medal in the Beijing Olympics. He firmly believes that the Chinese team has more hope and a better future than the Korean team.

At the news briefing after the semi-final game, a Korean journalist asked a question that aroused heated discussion. "We hear the Chinese call you 'China's Hiddink'. Do you like it?"

"No Chinese calls me Hiddink!" Kim Chang Back answered in a sonorous voice. "I'm Kim Chang Back, the hockey coach Kim Chang Back, and the Kim Chang Back that wins the respect of 1.3 billion Chinese people! Please tell the Koreans that the Chinese don't call me Hiddink. They only know me as Kim Chang Back." It is true; for most Chinese, it is only through the name of Kim Chang Back that they started to hear about and know about hockey.

At the Beijing Olympics the Chinese female hockey team led by Kim Chang Back beat the Korean team 6:1, which made the Korean journalists sigh: "Now Kim Chang Back is really a Chinese, by any standard." In fact, deep in his heart, Kim Chang Back loves his motherland deeply. He is a Korean for ever.

The 2002 Busan Asian Games was one that Kim Chang Back really wanted to participate in, for he would prove himself in his motherland and report to his fellow countrymen. He is always called a "devil" on the court, but actually he has rich feelings. In 1999, an irreconcilable conflict arose between Kim Chang Back, a man of strong character, and the Korean Hockey Association. So he was unemployed. Then the Chinese Hockey Association offered him a position and a brand-new stage. Ever since 1987, he started to observe the Chinese female hockey team and found until the late 1990s that they had made no great progress. But he knew why, and wished to fully display his talent on a new stage. Thus he accepted an invitation to coach the Chinese team with pleasure. "I want to show my ability to my fellow countrymen." He also wants to repay the Chinese for their appreciation and recognition.

Then the young Chinese female hockey team defeated the Korean hockey team—the champion of four Asian Games. His countrymen in Busan considered the victory of the Chinese team as Kim Chang Back's victory. Although there was criticism, he received more praise from the media. Later,

seeing the glorious victories that the Chinese female hockey team won, the Korean Hockey Association regretted losing such a great coach, and repeatedly invited him to go back to Korea. However, Kim Chang Back, who had forged an indissoluble bond with China and moved all his family here, refused.

"I'm not a Korean Hiddink, but a Chinese Kim Chang Back"—Old Kim's declaration moved numerous Chinese. The Chinese TV audience has long found that although he speaks Chinese with a thick accent, on the whole, his Chinese is quite fluent. Old Kim also said he almost forgets he is a Korean. Only when he produces his passport at the airports in China can he realize that he is actually a Korean. To have dinner together with the players, he tried hard to adapt himself to Chinese cuisine. Nine years ago, when he first went to Guangdong, he found caraway in every dish. Knowing that if he wouldn't eat coriandrum sativum, he would have great difficulty living in China, he then changed his taste. Now he would feel uneasy if there were no coriandrum sativum. Of course he still keeps his taste in kimchi. His wife can make perfect kimchi. Everyone who has tasted their homemade kimchi praises it, saying that it is much better than the "authentic Korean kimchi" in the supermarkets.

When the terrible earthquake shook Wenchuan in early 2008, the Chinese female hockey team was in Germany participating in the Championship Cup. Returning to China, Kim Chang Back, who no longer thinks of himself as a foreigner, immediately donated 100,000 yuan to the victims—almost one third of Kim's savings—even though all six members of his family are now living in China, including two college students, and all depend on his salary.

"Devil's training" makes the winning team

Some Chinese were once asked: "Your Chinese players are much weaker physically than the European and American players. What force supported you to run till the last minute?" In fact, they didn't know that this force was the result of cruel training. If you see the "devil's" training of the Chinese female hockey team, you'll know why they could achieve one miracle after another. With such training, it is natural that they win victories.

When Old Kim became the head coach of the Chinese female hockey team in January 2000, he said, "Physical strength is the weakest link in the Chinese team, but it is the basis on which all the tactics and techniques can be applied." But the players couldn't accept his "cruelty" at the beginning. Even the Chinese assistant coach disagreed with him sometimes. Yang Chao, director of the Hockey Department, said point-blank: "At first, since we had no such experience, we felt it difficult to agree with him about his training methods."

But within a short time, the success of Old Kim's team made everyone look at him with new eyes. Only three months later, the Chinese female hockey team gained the right to participate in the Sidney Olympics, it was to be their first Olympic appearance. Four months later, it finished in fifth place in the Olympics, whereas in 1999 when Kim Chang Back was invited to "make a thorough examination" of the Chinese team, it only ranked 20th in the world. "We spent about 50 percent of the five months preparing for the Olympics, improving tactics and techniques, and the other 50 percent mainly

on improving physical strength." said Kim. The Chinese team, which was always strong in agility but weak in strength, finally proved with its success that the several months' "devil's" training had really paid off.

The first time Kim met the team, he required the girls to call each other sisters, to avoid forming small groups. He forbade the players to call him "coach"; instead, he was to be called "Teacher" Kim. In this way, he established his dignity and authority as a teacher. He found a tree branch, polished it, and carved the two Chinese characters "Bi Sheng" (meaning "victory every time") on it. During training, he always held the branch, yelling at the players and hitting them with the "victory stick" or even kicking those who slackened off or made mistakes.

In Korea, players must absolutely obey the orders of the coaches, and the coaches may use every means, including beating and abuse, to stimulate the players. But in China, things are different, for we have a different culture. Although the Chinese players tried hard to bear it, and the Korean coach also had scruples, both sides felt that they couldn't coordinate. Later the Chinese leaders discussed it with Kim, and persuaded him to give up the stick. But the players, although there was no stick in his hand, still felt it was right beside them.

No, that's no good. Do it again.

The girls of the Chinese

female hockey team once said, "It was so hard that we even wanted to cry! The devil's training of Teacher Kim was almost cruel. One failure brought you punishment, not only punishment on you, but also on the whole team. Nobody was spared. Thus those making mistakes had to bear great pressure physically and psychologically." Before an exercise game, since their opponent was weaker than them, Kim Chang Back required they should win by ten points; one point less would mean 50 spurts as punishment. But they only scored one point, so Kim gave them nine groups of 50 spurts as punishment, which lasted till over 11 p.m. The girls' hearts still flutter with fear whenever this is mentioned.

Without self-confidence and the courage to act, you can never win, Kim Chang Back repeatedly told the players. "At first, when Teacher Kim told us 'I'll make you a top-class team',... we all thought he was boasting. But the truth is, his goals are reached one after another. Before the last Olympics, he made a survey in which no player dared to set the goal to be the first six, so he was very angry. He said, "we must have the confidence to win the first three, and only if we strive for this can we win."

Kim Chang Back found the Chinese were too shy to speak on the court, so the atmosphere was not hot enough. He said, "If you don't shout on the court, but just pass the ball, your teammate can't prepare in advance. You have mouths; why don't you shout?" But the players were not used to it, so Kim Chang Back started to punish them by making them run while shouting. Later the Chinese team was able to cooperate well, and they became more and more confident.

Kim Chang Back is a man of good order. His room is in as good order as his training plans, and he has clear lines of thinking. No matter how late

the training has finished, every evening he collects from the Internet the latest reports about hockey worldwide. He is definitely not a coach who only depends on devil-like training to make progress.

"Some day we could be the world champions, but this needs hard work," said Kim Chang Back. Racking his brains during the devil's training, this thin little old man became even thinner. But his eyes were still keen. During the first months, when he had to adapt himself to the new situation and coordinate with the players and others, Kim lost ten kg. in body weight.

Kim's players never slacken, nor do they dare, no matter whether he is around or not, as if his eyes were supervising them all the time.

The devil coach also has a gentle side

Kim Chang Back doesn't care if he is called "devil coach", rather, he takes pride in it. On the court he is a devil, but off the court he is like a kind father. In their years of training he has formed a relationship closer than that of a family with the players. He gives them presents on their birthdays; he carries those injured on his back to the hospital; and he spends most of his bonus on the girls. "They are just like my daughters," he said.

At the Busan Asian Games, just before the final between the Chinese and Korean female hockey teams, Kim Chang Back carried a bunch of fresh red roses and walked into the middle of the court, smiling. While the journalists thought he was going to present the flowers to the opponents, he walked straight to player No. 11 of the Chinese team, presented the roses with both hands, and gently kissed her on the cheek. In fact, it was the 100th international competition that senior player Tang Chunling would play. Old Kim ordered 100 red roses the day before, and presented them to her that day in memory of this special moment. The battle-hardened Tang Chunling was very excited, saying she would play well in this 100th game and realize her first Asia championship dream. She made it, and her dream came true.

Kim Chang Back is also a dutiful son. Once he answered a call when he was away from Beijing, training. The players then sensed something was wrong from his mood. He said that his mother had been ill but only told him when she was almost well again. He blamed himself for not being able to do his duty as a son. "Mother said, you have a great career, so don't worry about me. Besides, does it matter whether you come back or not?" He breathed a deep sigh. Like everyone else, he had been away from home for nine months to realize his Olympic dream with his players.

Although under great mental pressure, he tries to make the players relax by making fun of them sometimes. The players said, "We see him getting old and withered. In the leisure time of Sundays, when we helped him pull out his white hairs, we felt sorry. But he joked: Your teacher is getting old, because you always annoy me." Then laughter lightened their heavy hearts, but sorrow remained in the girls' hearts.

Kim Chang Back likes drinking liquor, especially Chinese distilled liquor. The girls always bring him famous liquor of their hometowns when they make trips home. Afraid that it might cost too much, he told them he loved "Xiaohutuxian" brand best, since it was cheap. Later, considering his work, he stopped drinking liquor just for the 2008 Beijing Olympics.

A true hero is not necessarily iron-hearted. Teacher Kim is a man with tender feelings. He said only when they won the championship would he drink to their victory. His students and the Chinese fans sincerely hope that

some day he can drink to his heart's content. In fact, after August 22, he was able to end his abstinence.

Teacher Kim and his family have settled down in China

After the Sidney Olympics, Kim moved his family to Beijing, and seemed to be going to settle down here. China has become his second home. But he often "went past his own house without even looking in". According to his wife Park Mi Kyung, she could meet him once a week when they were in Korea. But now in China, sometimes she cannot see him for months. Thanks to his able wife, who takes good care of everyone's life in his family, Old Kim can devote all his time and energy to training and matches without having to worry about his family.

When he first came to China, Old Kim liked listening to the Chinese song "The Moon of Mid-Autumn". Maybe this nostalgic song echoed his own mood. "The medal for military merit belongs to both you and me" in the words of this song might just be what old Kim wanted to sing to his wife. When he moved his whole family to China, he was still too busy to go home. Then he loved "Love Song of a Single Person". Probably he could relieve his nostalgia through singing this song.

No one knows a person better than his mother. Talking about her son, Kim's mother Ak Pil-sook wears a proud expression: "My son was born to achieve great success." But when talking about his temper, the old lady feels really worried: "My son is hot-tempered. Sometimes when the players don't train well he is even too worried to eat anything." She continued, "My son works as the coach of the Chinese team. If he can't work well, the whole family will be upset. Now he has won great success, and my grandsons and granddaughter are studying well at a Chinese university and at school, and so I feel really contented. I pray for him every day, hoping he can lead his team to a better future."

The two elder children of Kim Chang Back are now studying at Tsinghua University. The eldest son majors in biology while the second child, his daughter, studies in the Department of Chinese Language and literature. His youngest son is now in high school. Old Kim hopes he could learn Chinese well like his sons and daughter, and enter a famous university. He hopes his daughter may marry a Chinese, since most Chinese men take good care of their wives. But he thinks his son had better marry a Korean girl, for male chauvinism couldn't work on a Chinese wife.

His family has successfully merged with Chinese society and is living happily in China. Besides, he has many Korean friends in Beijing. He lives in Wangjing, which is like a Korean town and Korean language signs can be seen on goods in supermarkets and at bus stops, so that life is very convenient and they are too happy to miss their old life in Busan.

After the Olympics, Kim Chang Back plans to have a good rest, and tour China to enjoy the beautiful landscape. He is too tired, and his students and Chinese friends all hope he may take good care of himself. Of course we hope he will go on leading the Chinese female hockey team to win new glory!

By Kong Ning, Li Li, and Zong He
Translated by Zhang Chunhua
Photos provided by cnsphoto and www.sportsphoto.cn

图书在版编目（CIP）数据

老外的中国梦：英文／绿杨等著；杨耀华等译．
—北京：新世界出版社，2008.11
（中外文化交流系列）
ISBN 978-7-80228-841-6

I．老…　Ⅱ．①绿…②杨…　Ⅲ．①外国人－生平事迹－现代－英文
②中国－概况－英文　Ⅳ．K812.5　K92

中国版本图书馆 CIP 数据核字（2008）第 177032 号

Dreaming Big in China
老外的中国梦

作　　者：绿　杨　等
策　　划：李淑娟　张海鸥
翻　　译：杨耀华　等
责任编辑：李淑娟
英文改稿：Paul White
英文审定：徐明强
封面设计：王天义
装帧设计：清鑫工作室
责任印制：李一鸣　黄厚清
出版发行：新世界出版社
社　　址：北京市西城区百万庄大街 24 号（100037）
总编室电话：＋ 86 10 6899 5424　68326679（传真）
发行部电话：＋ 86 10 6899 5968　68998705（传真）
本社中文网址：http://www.nwp.cn
本社英文网址：http://www.newworld-press.com
版权部电子信箱：frank@nwp.com.cn
版权部电话：＋ 86 10 6899 6306
印刷：北京外文印刷厂
经销：新华书店
开本：787 × 1092　1/16
字数：180 千字　印张：19.25
版次：2009 年 1 月第 1 版　2009 年 1 月北京第 1 次印刷
书号：ISBN 978-7-80228-841-6
定价：78.00 元